JAPANESE CORE WORDS AND PHRASES

Things you Can't Find in a Dictionary

JAPANESE CORE WORDS AND PHRASES

Things you Can't Find in a Dictionary

Kazuko Shoji

KODANSHA INTERNATIONAL
Tokyo • New York • London

Previously published as *Core Words and Phrases: Things You Can't Find in a Dictionary* in Kodansha International's Power Japanese series.

NOTE TO THE READER
Cross-references to "Shoji" in the text refer to *Basic Connections: Making Your Japanese Flow* by Kakuko Shoji (Kodansha International)

Distributed in the United States by Kodansha America, Inc., and in the United Kingdom and continental Europe by Kodansha Europe Ltd.

Published by Kodansha International Ltd., 17–14 Otowa 1-chome, Bunkyo-ku, Tokyo 112–8652, and Kodansha America, Inc.

Copyright © 1999 by Kakuko Shoji.
All rights reserved. Printed in Japan.
ISBN 978–4–7700–2774–0

First edition, 1999
First trade paperback edition, 2001
15 14 13 12 11 10 09 08 07   15 14 13 12 11 10 9 8

www.kodansha-intl.com

CONTENTS

PART 2: IDIOMATIC EXPRESSIONS

Preface

Students of Japanese often say that Japanese is difficult to learn because of kanji, and it is certainly true that kanji present a formidable obstacle to beginning students. But once students have gained some facility with the language, most realize that kanji are not the only problem. At the intermediate or advanced level, what is required are means of expression that are culturally textured and contextually interwoven, which I imagine is true of any foreign language. At this stage, not only must students increase their general vocabulary and store of idiomatic expressions, but also realize that previously learned words and phrases must be transformed from locutions that are simple and fixed in meaning into ones that are multidimensional and many-layered. This book is an effort to help students do precisely that.

In my previous book in the Power Japanese series, *Basic Connections: Making Your Japanese Flow*, I took up relatively basic problems that my students often had trouble with in the classroom. In this book, I have chosen to treat issues that often appear in textbooks and other publications for intermediate and advanced students, such as sentence structure, idiomatic usage, and conjunctions. In particular, I have focused on expressions, such as *ko-so-a-do* words, whose meaning changes radically according to context. Further, I have made an effort to include problems that appear in the second and third levels of the Japanese Language Proficiency Test.

In compiling and publishing this book, I have received the cooperation of many people. Among them I would particularly like to thank the graduate students in Chinese philosophy and history at the University of Hawaii as well as my colleagues and family for their unstinting support. I would also like to thank Michael Brase and Shigeyoshi Suzuki of Kodansha International for their assistance.

Kakuko Shoji
1999

まえがき

　日本語のクラスなどで、よく「日本語は漢字があるから難しい」という学生に出会います。たしかに漢字は初学者にとって大きなハードルになっていることでしょう。しかし「やっと日本語が使える」というレベルを越えるころになると、日本語を難しくしているものは、漢字ばかりではないことに気付くはずです。これはどんな言語においても同じではないかと思いますが、中級、上級と進めば、より文化に密着した、ハイコンテクストな表現を学ぶ必要が生じます。従って、より広範囲の語彙、慣用句などを学ばなければならないとともに、既に学んだ単語や表現が、実は一義的、固定的なものではなく、状況に応じて多義的、重層的に意味を変化させるということを認識しなければなりません。

　前回出版いたしました『Basic Connections』は、私の学生がよく間違ったり戸惑ったりする問題の中で比較的基本的な問題を扱っていますが、本書では中級から上級の初めに使用する教科書や問題集に登場する構文、慣用表現、接続表現などのうち、学生が習得に苦労するもの—例えば前後関係によって大幅に意味の変化する「こ・そ・あ・ど」系の表現—などを取り上げてみました。また日本語能力試験の二級、三級の問題に出てくる項目もできるだけ入れるようにしています。

　本書を刊行するにあたり多くの方々にご協力をいただきました。有意義で示唆に富む問題点を提供してくれたハワイ大学の中国哲学、歴史学の大学院生たち、終始変わらぬ支援で私を励ましてくださった同僚の方たちや家族、そしてこの本を出版する機会を与えてくださった講談社インターナショナルの編集者マイケル・ブレイズさん、鈴木重好さん、みなさまにお礼を申し上げたいと思います。

1999年
庄司香久子

PART

1

こそあど WORDS

This part of the book deals with so-called こそあど words, which are words that indicate either physical or psychological distance. Some are pronouns, some adjectives, some adverbs, and some change functions according to context. The easiest to understand are the demonstrative pronouns. A pronoun, of course, is a word that stands in place of a noun or a noun phrase. For example, in "The man is mad, but he is happy," "he" stands for "man." A demonstrative pronoun is a pronoun that points to something in terms of distance from the speaker. "This" and "that" are demonstrative pronouns in the sentence "This is my chair; that is yours."

Japanese has three types of demonstrative pronouns: これ, which indicates something close to the speaker or close to both the speaker and the other party to the conversation; それ, which indicates something at a distance from the speaker but close to the other party; and あれ, which indicates something distant from both parties. You will have noticed that the first syllable in these words corresponds to the first three syllables in the term "こそあど words." The last syllable, ど, would be represented by どれ in the list given here. どれ, however, is not used to indicate distance but refers to something indefinite or indicates a question; in that sense,

どれ and the other ど words are somewhat different from the first three types of こそあど words.

Aside from the fact that こそあど words indicate three types of distance compared to the two indicated by "this" and "that" in English, one of the major problems represented by こそあど words is that they indicate psychological as well as physical distance. This will be the principal focus of the entries in this part of the book. Another difficulty is that こそあど words are used in idiomatic ways that are not easily understood from their surface meaning alone. For these reasons, we have chosen to take up a number of the more difficult, but also common, usages and show how they should be properly understood.

こそあど words have four main categories, and each category is comprised of six words. That is to say, the initial syllables are followed by suffixes that indicate what the word has reference to—whether a thing, a person, a direction, or something else. Below is a listing of all こそあど words, with suffixed examples listed under the main divisions.

こ = close to the speaker or close to both speaker and the other conversant

    これ = this (thing, person, or event)

    ここ = this (place or time)

    こちら or こっち = this (direction, alternative, or person)

    この = this (thing, person, or event)

    こんな = this (kind of)

    こう = this (way or manner of)

そ = distant from the speaker and close to the other conversant

    それ = that (thing, person, or event)

そこ = that (place or time)

そちら or そっち = that (direction, alternative, or person)

その = that (thing, person, or event)

そんな = that (kind of)

そう = that (way or manner of)

あ = distant from both the speaker and the other conversant

あれ = that over there (thing, person, or event)

あそこ = that over there (place or time)

あちら or あっち = that over there (direction, alternative, or person)

あの = that over there (thing, person, or event)

あんな = that over there (kind of)

ああ = that over there (way or manner of)

ど = indefinite or interrogative

どれ = what (thing, person, or event)

どこ = what (place, location, or position)

どちら or どっち = what (direction, alternative, or person)

どの = what (thing, person, or event)

どんな = what (kind of)

どう = what (way or manner of)

In the following discussion こそあど words are taken up not in the order given above but rather in an order that facilitates their discussion.

あ Words

あ words are commonly employed when something has slipped one's mind and cannot be recalled no matter how hard one tries. In such cases, the speaker uses an あ word to get the other party's help. The other person may also respond with an あ word if he/she cannot remember either.

あれ

あれ is typically used when trying to recall a name, a place, or the like.

> A: ほら、<u>あれ</u>!
>
> *Hora, are!*
>
> Listen … That! (What was the name of the song? Oh, I forgot.) Don't you remember it?

> B: <u>あれ</u>？　<u>あれ</u>、ビートルズよね。ええとねえ……<u>あれ</u>……なんだっけなあ？
>
> *Are? Are, Bītoruzu yo ne. Eeto nē … are … nan da kke nā?*
>
> That? That's a Beetles' song, isn't it? Well … that … What was the name? (I can't remember either.)

> A: 去年、コーヒーのおいしい喫茶店に行ったでしょう。<u>あれ</u>、どこだっけ？
>
> *Kyonen, kōhi no oishii kissaten ni itta deshō. Are, doko da kke?*
>
> We went to a coffee shop last year that had good coffee. Where was that? (Do you remember?)

> B: ええっと、あそこはね……<u>あれ</u>、渋谷だったよね。あ、思い出した！　<u>あれ</u>、駅前の喫茶店だよ。
>
> *Eetto, asoko wa ne … are, Shibuya datta yo ne. A, omoidashita! Are, ekimae no kissaten da yo.*
>
> Let me see … That was … That was in Shibuya, right? Oh, I remember! That was the coffee shop in front of the station.

あれっきり／あれ以来

あれっきり and あれ以来（いらい）, both of which can be translated as "since then," refer to a time that is known from context but not specified.

A: 正子さん、今どうしてるか、知っている？

Masako-san, ima dō shite 'ru ka, shitte iru?

Do you know how Masako's doing now?

B: 去年会ったけど、<u>あれっきり／あれ以来</u>、音沙汰がないの。どうしてるかしら。

Kyonen atta kedo, are kkiri/are irai, otosata ga nai no. Dō shite 'ru kashira.

I met her last year, but I haven't heard a word from her since then. I wonder how she's doing.

あれだけ／あんなに

Both of these mean "to that extent" or "to that degree" and refer to something that is known from context but is not specified.

A: 電話するのが遅かったもので、切符、買えなかったんです。

Denwa suru no ga osokatta mono de, kippu, kaenakatta n' desu.

Because I called late, I couldn't get a ticket.

B: だから、<u>あれだけ／あんなに</u>早くしなさいって言ったのに。

Dakara, are dake/anna ni hayaku shinasai tte itta no ni.

That's why I told you so many times to do it earlier.

あの／例の

あの refers to something that happened in the past, the knowledge or experience of which is shared by the people engaged in the conversation. 例の may be used in much the same sense.

A: <u>例の</u>入社試験、どうだった？　うまくいった？

Rei no nyūsha shiken, dō datta? Umaku itta?

How was that company's hiring examination (the one you were talking about)? Did you do well?

B: <u>あれ</u>？　不採用。<u>あの</u>試験、めちゃくちゃ難しかったのよ。

Are? Fusaiyō. Ano shiken, mechakucha muzukashikatta no yo.

That? I didn't get the job. The examination was awfully difficult.

あれやこれや／ああ言えばこう言うで／あちこち

あ words are sometimes used with こ words to refer to a random thing, place, matter, and so on.

<u>あれやこれや</u>と、することが多くて疲れる。

Are ya kore ya to suru koto ga ōkute tsukareru.

What with this and that, there are so many things to do I get tired out.

あの人は、<u>ああ言えばこう言うで</u>、理屈ばかり言うので皆に 嫌われている。

Ano hito wa, ā ieba kō iu de, rikutsu bakari iu no de mina ni kirawarete iru.

He is always rationalizing and has a reason for everything. That's why no one likes him.

<u>あちこち</u>探してみたが、彼の気に入るような家はなかなか見つからない。

Achikochi sagashite mita ga, kare no ki ni iru yō na ie wa nakanaka mitsukaranai.

I've looked here and there, but it's hard to find the kind of house that might be to his liking.

あの人／あいつ／うちの人／うちの奴

In referring to a person who is within sight but at some distance from the speaker and listener, あの人 (ひと) "that person" can be used: e.g., あの人は誰 (だれ) ですか (Who is the person over there?). However, あの人 can also be used to refer to someone close to, or intimate with, the speaker, such as a spouse or friend. In this sense, men speaking casually are more likely to use あいつ than あの人. When referring specifically to a spouse, women can also use うちの人 instead あの人 when referring to their husbands, and men うちの奴 (やつ) instead of あいつ when referring to their wives.

A: どうして、この真冬にアラスカなんかに行くの？

Dōshite, kono mafuyu ni Arasuka nanka ni iku no?

Why are you going to a place like Alaska right in the middle of the winter?

B: あの人がどうしても一緒に行こうって言うから。

Ano hito ga dōshite mo issho ni ikō tte iu kara.

Because he (my husband, boyfriend, etc.) insists that I go with him.

A: 悪ぶってるけど、あいつ、根はとてもいい奴なんだよ。

Warubutte 'ru kedo, aitsu, ne wa totemo ii yatsu nan da yo.

He acts tough, but he's really good at heart.

B: でも、いじわるなことばかり言うから、嫌い。

Demo, ijiwaru na koto bakari iu kara, kirai.

Still I don't like him because he's always saying mean things.

A: 今週の週末、長野にスキーに行くんだけど、一緒に行かない？

Konshū no shūmatsu, Nagano ni sukī ni iku n' da kedo, issho ni ikanai?

We're going to Nagano to ski this weekend. Want to come along?

B: 行きたいねえ。でも、先に<u>うちの奴</u>に聞いてみないと。

Ikitai nē. Demo, saki ni uchi no yatsu ni kiite minai to.

I'd really like to go. But I'll have to ask my wife first.

(male)

B: 行きたい。でも、先に<u>うちの人</u>に聞いてみないと。

Ikitai. Demo, saki ni uchi no hito ni kiite minai to.

I want to go. But I'll have to ask my husband first.

(female)

あんな

あんな ("that kind of") sometimes shows negative feelings on the speaker's part.

<u>あんな</u>人が好きだなんて信じられない。

Anna hito ga suki da nante shinjirarenai.

I cannot believe that you like that kind of (terrible, cheap, no good) person.

<u>あんな</u>の、ただでもお断りよ。

Anna no, tada de mo okotowari yo.

I'd refuse that kind of thing even if it were free.

こ Words

こ words usually refer to something or someone spatially closer to the speaker than to the listener, or spatially close to both the speaker and the listener, as in the following dialogue.

A: <u>これ</u>は何ですか。

Kore wa nan desu ka.

What is this (close to me/in front of us)?

B: それは、本です。／<u>これ</u>は、本です。

Sore wa, hon desu. / Kore wa, hon desu.

That (close to you) is a book. / This (in front of us) is a book.

However, こ words are also used in relation to time, degree, limits, and the like, as perceived by the speaker. こんなところ／こんなもの is used to sum up, estimate, or compromise.

<u>これ</u>でいい？

Kore de ii?

Is this (limit, amount, price, etc.) OK?

<u>これ</u>までにいくつ漢字を習っていますか。

Kore made ni ikutsu kanji o naratte imasu ka.

How many *kanji* have you learned up to now?

こ words can refer to something that has just been mentioned (see first example below) or something that will be mentioned immediately after the こ word (second example below).

最近、<u>間違った英語を書いた商品をよく見かける</u>が、<u>これ</u>は無視するわけには行かない、由々しき問題である。

Saikin, machigatta eigo o kaita shōhin o yoku mikakeru ga, kore wa mushi suru wake ni wa ikanai, yuyushiki mondai de aru.

These days, you often come across merchandise with mistaken English on it. This is a serious problem that cannot be ignored.

昨日、<u>こんな</u>ことがありました。<u>知らない人から電話があったのですが、その人は、突然私の家を売ってほしいと言うのです。</u>

Sakujitsu, konna koto ga arimashita. Shiranai hito kara denwa ga atta no desu ga, sono hito wa, totsuzen watashi no ie o utte hoshii to iu no desu.

You can't guess what happened yesterday (Yesterday this kind of thing happened). I got a telephone call from a stranger, and out of the blue he says he wants me to sell him my house.

こんなところ／こんなもの, literally meaning "this kind of place" and "this kind of thing," might be paraphrased as "this is about where we stand" and "this is about it." They are used to sum up a discussion or an observation, to offer a compromise position, or to make an offer that the speaker feels is the best that can be made under the circumstances.

まあ、<u>こんなところ</u>だね。

Maa, konna tokoro da ne.

Well, this is about it (i.e., I think I've covered everything; I think that's all I have to say at the moment; I think this is about the best offer I can make).

まあ、彼にできるのは、<u>こんなもの</u>だろうね。

Maa, kare ni dekiru no wa, konna mono darō ne.

I don't think we can expect him to do any better than this.

そんなところ and そんなもの can be used in much the same way. However, whereas with こんなところ and こんなもの the speaker is presenting his own summation or opinion, with そんなところ and そんなもの the speaker is agreeing with the summation or opinion presented by the other party to the conversation or is summing up his or her own view of the matter that the other party has apparently agreed with.

A: 今度のコンパの会費は、10ドルぐらいまででしょうね。

Kondo no konpa no kaihi wa, jūdoru gurai made deshō ne.

I think the party fee shouldn't be over ten dollars. What do you think?

B: まあ、<u>そんなところ</u>だろうね。

Maa, sonna tokoro darō ne.

Yeah, that's about it, I guess. / You're probably right.

A: 人生なんて、なかなか思うようにはいかないもんなん だって、やっと分かったわ。

Jinsei nante, nakanaka omou yō ni wa ikanai mon nan datte, yatto wakatta wa.

Life doesn't go as easily as expected. I have finally realized that.

B: そう、そんなものなんだよ。

Sō, sonna mono nan da yo.

Yes, that's about the size of it.

この間（あいだ）／この間（かん）

Although these two look alike because of the kanji used, they have different meanings. このあいだ means "the other day," referring to a time in the past but within the speaker's recent experience. このかん, on the other hand, means "the time between the two events in question." It is often followed by わずか or たったの ("only/as little as/no more than"), indicating that the interval in question was of short duration.

A: この間（あいだ）は、おみやげをありがとうございました。

Kono aida wa, omiyage o arigatō gozaimashita.

Thank you for the gift you gave me the other day.

B: いいえ。気に入っていただけてうれしいです。

Iie. Ki ni itte itadakete ureshii desu.

You're welcome. I'm glad you like it.

A: 目を覚まして、支度をして、家を飛び出して、バスに乗ったのが、八時ちょうど……この間（かん）、わずか／たったの十五分。すごいでしょ。

Me o samashite, shitaku o shite, ie o tobidashite, basu ni notta no ga, hachiji chōdo ... kono kan, wazuka/tatta no jūgofun. Sugoi desho.

I woke up, got ready, rushed out of the house, and got on the bus at exactly 8 o'clock ... All in only 15 minutes. Pretty amazing, huh?

B: 本当？　信じられないわ。

Hontō? Shinjirarenai wa.

Really? I can't believe it.

この頃（ごろ）／この頃（ころ）

この頃（ごろ）and この頃（ころ）are often confused, especially when they are written with kanji. They sound alike, but they are not interchangeable. このごろ simply means "recently," while このころ means "at about this time." It refers to a specific point in time in a specific context and is often used in stories, novels, or narrations. For instance, something happened at a certain place, and at about the same time something else happened at another place.

A: このごろ、お父さん、機嫌が悪いんだけど、何かあったの？

Kono goro, otōsan, kigen ga warui n' da kedo, nani ka atta no?

These days Dad is very edgy/in a bad mood. What happened?

B: 分からないけど、きっと仕事が忙しくて疲れてるんでしょ。

Wakaranai kedo, kitto shigoto ga isogashikute tsukarete 'ru n' desho.

I don't know. He's probably tired because he's busy at work.

六月の中旬ごろ、日本列島はうっとうしい梅雨の季節に入るが、一方北海道が美しい花の季節を迎えるのも、またこのころなのである。

Rokugatsu no chūjun goro, Nihon-rettō wa uttōshii tsuyu no kisetsu ni hairu ga, ippō Hokkaidō ga utsukushii hana no kisetsu o mukaeru no mo, mata kono koro na no de aru.

About the middle of June, the dreary rainy season starts in the Japan archipelago. However, it is also at this time that Hokkaido welcomes the beautiful season of flowers.

通報を受けた警部たちがアジトに急行したが、犯人達はこのころ、すでに国外に逃亡していた。

Tsūhō o uketa keibu-tachi ga ajito ni kyūkō shita ga, hannin-tachi wa kono koro, sude ni kokugai ni tōbō shite ita.

Detectives rushed to the hideout as soon as they received the information, but by this time the suspects had already fled abroad.

ここ

ここ, when it is followed by a time word such as 一年 "one year" or しばらく "for a while," refers not to a place but to a current point in time. For instance, 一年 can be any one year, while ここ一年 means "this past (one) year." このところ may replace ここしばらく (see このところ, below).

> ここしばらく、暖かい日が続いたが、また急に気温が下がって夕べから雪になった。
>
> *Koko shibaraku, atatakai hi ga tsuzuita ga, mata kyū ni kion ga sagatte yūbe kara yuki ni natta.*
>
> We've had warm weather now for a while, but the temperature suddenly went down and last evening we had snow.

> ここ一年、忙しくてどこにも行けなかったけど、来年こそは休暇をとって旅行したいと思っています。
>
> *Koko ichinen, isogashikute doko ni mo ikenakatta kedo, rainen koso wa kyūka o totte ryokō shitai to omotte imasu.*
>
> I couldn't go anywhere this past year because I was so busy, but next year I'm definitely going to take a vacation and travel.

このところ

このところ is not interchangeable with このごろ, which means "recently." このところ refers to a time period shortly before the present time in a particular situation, while このごろ refers to a more general time period and situation. For instance, このごろの若 (わか) い者 (もの) は ("young people these day") is a phrase often heard when older people criticize the behavior of the younger generation, so このところ may sound awkward if used in this phrase. (See also このごろ.)

このところ、雨の日ばかり続くので、うんざりしています。

Kono tokoro, ame no hi bakari tsuzuku no de, unzari shite imasu.

Lately, we've had nothing but rainy days. It's so depressing,

このところ、全然会わなかったけど、どこかに行ってたの。

Kono tokoro, zenzen awanakatta kedo, doko ka ni itte 'ta no.

I haven't seen you around at all lately. Were you off someplace?

チャーリーは、このところお母さんの具合が悪化しているとの知らせを受けて、帰国しました。

Chārī wa, kono tokoro okāsan no guai ga akka shite iru to no shirase o ukete, kikoku shimashita.

Charley went back to his home country, having learned that his mother's condition had recently gotten worse.

これから

これから ("from here") refers to two different time points: "right now" and "from now on."

では、これから試験を始めます。

Dewa, kore kara shiken o hajimemasu.

Now we will start the examination.

A: すみません。お借りした花瓶、うっかり落として割っちゃったんです。

Sumimasen. Okari shita kabin, ukkari otoshite watchatta n' desu.

I'm sorry. I carelessly dropped the vase I borrowed from you and broke it.

B: 高いものじゃないから、いいけど、<u>これから</u>は、もっ
と気をつけてね。

*Takai mono ja nai kara, ii kedo, kore kara wa, motto ki o
tsukete ne.*

It wasn't expensive, so it's all right, but be more careful
from now on.

この先（さき）

この先 may replace これから when it means "from now on"
or "in the future":

こんなに円安が続いたら、<u>これから／この先</u>、輸出入に
頼っている企業は大変だろう。

*Konna ni enyasu ga tsuzuitara, kore kara/kono saki,
yushutsunyū ni tayotte iru kigyō wa taihen darō.*

If the yen continues as weak as it is, companies depend-
ing on foreign trade are going to have a hard time
from now on.

先 sometimes confuses students, because while it can mean
"before in time" or "before in place," it can also refer to a
point, in time or space, which comes later. Here are examples of both usages.

お<u>先</u>に（失礼します）。

Osaki ni (shiturei shimasu).

(Excuse me, but) I must go/do it now (ahead of you).

<u>先</u>日はどうも（ありがとうございました）。

Senjitsu wa dōmo (arigatō gozaimashita).

Thank you for the other day.

<u>この先</u>、彼等はどこに住むのだろうか。

Kono saki, karera wa doko ni sumu no darō ka.

I wonder where they are going to live from now on.

銀行は、デパートの先です。

Ginkō wa, depāto no saki desu.

The bank is beyond the department store.

この分だと／この分なら／この分では

All three mean "If this situation/condition goes on like this." However, the implications are different. この分なら is used to imply that the outcome of the existing state, condition, or action will be good and favorable. この分だと, on the other hand, commonly introduces an undesirable or unfavorable result. この分では may be used interchangeably with この分だと, but here the outcome is rather uncertain. It commonly takes sentence endings such as かもしれない and ではないか.

A: あしたの天気、どうかな。テニスの試合があるんだけど。

Ashita no tenki, dō ka na. Tenisu no shiai ga aru n' da kedo.

I wonder what the weather will be like tommorow. We have a tennis match.

B: この分なら、大丈夫よ。晴れてきてるから。

Kono bun nara, daijōbu yo. Harete kite 'ru kara.

At this rate, it should be all right. It has started to clear up.

A: おじいさん、どんな具合ですか。

Ojiisan, donna guai desu ka.

How is your grandfather?

B: お医者さんが、この分だともう駄目かもしれないって。

Oisha-san ga, kono bun da to mō dame kamo shirenai tte.

His doctor said, if the unstable condition continues, he might not make it.

A: あの裁判、いつまで続くのかしら。

Ano saiban, itsu made tsuzuku no kashira.

I wonder how long that trial will go on?

B: <u>この分では</u>、どうなるか分からないよ。二、三年はだ
らだら続くのかもしれないね。

*Kono bun de wa, dō naru ka wakaranai yo. Ni, sannen
wa daradara tsuzuku no kamo shirenai ne.*

If it goes like this, you just can't tell. It may drag on for
a couple more years.

これでも

これでも is often used when the speaker wishes to protest
against what someone has said but tries not to sound too
harsh. Literally the meaning is "even being this," but the
connotation is "even though things may appear this way
(which to you seems somehow insufficient or substan-
dard)." The speaker then goes on to lodge a protest or state
a contrary opinion.

A: 今日、君の誕生日だよね。四十になったんだっけ？

Kyō, kimi no tanjōbi da yo ne. Yonjū ni natta n' da kke?

Today is your birthday, isn't it? Are you 40 now?

B: 失礼ね！　まだ四十になんかなっていません。<u>これで
も</u>、三十五です。

*Shitsurei ne! Mada yonjū ni nanka natte imasen. Kore de
mo, sanjūgo desu.*

How rude! I haven't reached anything like 40 yet.
Despite appearances, I'm only 35.

A: 遊んでばかりいないで、もっとまじめに勉強しなさい。

Asonde bakari inai de, motto majime ni benkyō shinasai.

Don't keep fooling around all the time. You've got to
study harder.

B: <u>これでも</u>、一生懸命やってるんだから、がみがみ言わ
ないでよ。

*Kore de mo, isshō-kenmei yatte 'ru n da kara, gamigami
iwanai de yo.*

In spite of what you may think, I'm doing my level best,
so stop nagging.

これでも may also be used in scolding, accusing, or evaluating something or someone negatively. According to the situation それ and あれ may replace これ.

A: なんか安っぽい感じね。

Nanka yasuppoi kanji ne.

I don't know why, but it looks cheap.

B: そんなこと、言わないで。<u>これでも</u>十万円はしたんだから……

Sonna koto, iwanai de. Kore de mo jūman-en wa shita n' da kara ...

Oh, don't say that. It may not look like much, but I did pay ¥100,000 for it.

<u>それでも</u>女の子なの？　女の子なら、もっと口のきき方に気をつけなさい。

Sore de mo onna no ko na no? Onna no ko nara, motto kuchi no kikikata ni ki o tsukenasai.

A girl, behaving like that? If you are in fact a girl, watch how you speak.

A: あの新しい先生、頼りなさそうに見えるけど大丈夫かな。

Ano atarashii sensei, tayori nasasō ni mieru kedo daijōbu ka na.

That new teacher doesn't look very reliable. I wonder if he'll work out.

B: 大丈夫でしょ。<u>あれでも</u>一流大学出身なんだから。

Daijōbu desho. Are de mo ichiryū daigaku shusshin nan da kara.

I suppose so. He may not look like much, but he did graduate from one of the best colleges.

これまで／これっきり

Both これまで and これっきり mean "this is it" or "this is the end." However, the situations to which the expressions refer are different. In case of これまで, the phrase refers to an ending point that the speaker cannot change, like the outcome of one's fate or luck. これっきり, on the other hand, refers to an end that was intentionally made by the speaker, who may still cancel it. In other words, the speaker may voluntarily change the time of ending.

A: 彼の会社、倒産したんだって？

Kare no kaisha, tōsan shita n' da tte?

I heard that his company went bankrupt. Is that right?

B: ええ。『残念ながら、僕の実業家としての生命は<u>これまで</u>だ』って言ってましたよ。

Ee. "Zannen nagara, boku no jitsugyō-ka toshite no seimei wa kore made da" tte itte 'mashita yo.

Yes, it's true. He said, "To my regret, my life as a businessman has come to an end."

今日の講義は<u>これまで</u>にします。また明日続きをやりましょう。

Kyō no kōgi wa kore made ni shimasu. Mata ashita tsuzuki o yarimashō.

I'll end today's lecture here. Let's continue tomorrow.

A: もう<u>これっきり</u>よ。そんなに食べたらお腹こわしますよ。

Mō korekkiri yo. Sonna ni tabetara onaka kowashimasu yo.

No more for you. If you eat too much, you'll get a stomachache.

B: お願い。もう一つだけ。

Onegai. Mō hitotsu dake.

Please. Just one more.

A: しようがないわね。じゃあ、もう一つだけ。でも本当に<u>これっきり</u>ですよ。

Shiyō ga nai wa ne. Jā, mō hitotsu dake. Demo hontō ni korekkiri desu yo.

Oh, well. I'll give you one more, but that's all.

これといった

This expression, which might be literally translated as "like this," is followed by a negative verb and indicates that there is nothing special or particular about the noun that the phrase modifies.

> お彼には、<u>これといった</u>趣味がない。強いて言えば、仕事が彼の趣味だと言えるだろう。
>
> *Kare ni wa, kore to itta shumi ga nai. Shiite ieba, shigoto ga kare no shumi da to ieru darō.*
>
> He doesn't have any particular hobby. If I had to name one, I would probably say it was his work.

> ジミーは、<u>これといった</u>取り柄のある人ではないけれど、なぜかみんなに好かれている。
>
> *Jimi wa, kore to itta torie no aru hito de wa nai keredo, naze ka minna ni sukarete iru.*
>
> Jimmy doesn't have any particular strong points to speak of, but for some reason everybody likes him.

To modify a verb, これといって is used in place of これといった.

> A: いらっしゃい。しばらくね。今日は、どんなご用件？
>
> *Irasshai. Shibaraku ne. Kyō wa, donna goyōken?*
>
> Hi! I haven't seen you for a long time. What can I do for you today?

> B: <u>これといって</u>、別に用はないんだけど、ちょっとあなたに会いたくなったから。
>
> *Kore to itte, betsu ni yō wa nai n' da kedo, chotto anata ni aitaku natta kara.*
>
> I don't have any special business to speak of. I just wanted to see you.

そ Words

そ words often refer to an aforementioned statement (see Shoji pp. 34–36).

それは／それが

As seen in the following examples, それ can also refer to a later statement. This is often used in the beginning of a documentary, recollection, or a detective story.

> <u>それは</u>、あまりにも突然の出来事だった。横転したレーサーカーのタイヤが自分たちの上に落ちてくるなんて、一体だれが予想できただろう。

Sore wa, amari ni mo totsuzen no dekigoto datta. Ōten shita rēsākā no taiya ga jibun-tachi no ue ni ochite kuru nante, ittai dare ga yosō dekita darō.

The accident happened all too suddenly. Who would have imagined that the tires from the colliding race cars would come falling down upon them?

> <u>それは</u>、うれしいニュースだった。会いたいと思っていた友人が休暇で上京するというのだ。

Sore wa, ureshii nyūsu datta. Aitai to omotte ita yūjin ga kyūka de jōkyō suru to iu no da.

It was happy news. A friend I had wanted to see would be coming to Tokyo on vacation.

> A: どうしたの？　スカートが泥だらけじゃない。

Dō shita no? Sukāto ga doro darake ja nai.

What happened? Your skirt is covered with mud.

> B: <u>それがね</u>。雨上がりの道を通ってたら、後ろから車が来て……。

Sore ga ne. Ameagari no michi o tōtte 'tara, ushiro kara kuruma ga kite ...

Well, you see, I was walking down this street after the rain had stopped and a car came up from behind ...

それならそうと／それならそれで

These expressions might be literally translated as "if that, even so" and paraphrased as "even so, still," indicating that even given certain disadvantageous circumstances, something could still have been done to alleviate the situation. They are commonly used when a speaker wants to complain or to show frustration, disappointment, or anger about something that another party did carelessly, improperly, or inconsiderately. The sentence containing the phrase often ends in のに, はず, or the like. そんならそうと／そんならそれで are colloquial equivalents.

<u>それならそれで</u>、もっと早く手の打ちようがあった<u>はず</u>です。

Sore nara sore de, motto hayaku te no uchiyō ga atta hazu desu.

Even so (even if that is true), there must have been something you could have done earlier.

<u>そんならそうと</u>、早く言えばいい<u>のに</u>。どうして今まで言わなかったの？

Sonnara sō to, hayaku ieba ii no ni. Dōshite ima made iwanakatta no?

If that's the way it is, you should have told me earlier. Why did you keep it to yourself till now?

<u>それならそれで</u>、そうと言ってくだされ<u>ば</u>よかったんですよ。

Sonnara sore de, sō to itte kudasareba yokatta n' desu yo.

If that's the case, you should have told me so.

それこそ

こそ is a particle used to intensify the preceding word or statement, which in this case is それ. Here, それ refers to a preceding statement. The whole phrase is used to point out the degree or extent of the effect, or result of, what is mentioned in the preceding statement. The statement following the phrase spells out the degree or result.

彼にそんなことを言ったら、<u>それこそ</u>大変なことになるよ。

Kare ni sonna koto o ittara, sore koso taihen na koto ni naru yo.

If you said something like that to him, there would be trouble for sure.

その痛さったら、<u>それこそ</u>言葉では言い表せないぐらい。

Sono itasa ttara, sore koso kotoba de wa iiarawasenai gurai.

The pain of it—it just can't be expressed in words.

沖縄の海の色は、<u>それこそ</u>目が覚めるような青さだった。

Okinawa no umi no iro wa, sore koso me ga sameru yō na aosa datta.

The color of the sea of Okinawa—it was a truly brilliant and dazzling blue (lit., a blue that opens the eyes).

そういえば

This phrase might be literally translated as "if you (or someone) says that" or "if that is said," but in actual usage the literal meaning of "say" has been almost entirely lost. The connotation is that something (said, heard, felt) has lead by association to another thought, which leads the speaker to recall some matter from his or her memory.

A: あの頃、英語のクラスは人気があったから教室はいつもいっぱいだったよね。

Ano koro, eigo no kurasu wa ninki ga atta kara kyōshitsu wa itsumo ippai datta yo ne.

The English class then was popular, so the classroom was always full, wasn't it.

B: <u>そういえば</u>、あのクラスに淳子さんっていう人、いたでしょう。今どうしてるかしら。

Sō ieba, ano kurasu ni Junko-san tte iu hito, ita deshō. Ima dō shite 'ru kashira.

That reminds me. There was a girl named Junko in the class, right? I wonder what she is doing now.

A: 子供のころ、小さな白黒テレビでよくアメリカのホームドラマを見たね。

Kodomo no koro, chiisana shirokuro-terebi de yoku Amerika no hōmu-dorama o mita ne.

When we were kids, we used to watch dramas centered around American family life on small black and white televisions.

B: <u>そういえば</u>、あのころはカラーテレビなんかなかったんだよね。

Sō ieba, ano koro wa karā-terebi nanka nakatta n' da yo ne.

Now that you mention it, there wasn't any color TV in those days.

そうそう

そう literally means "it is like that," and そうそう is a simple repetition for emphasis. Both are commonly used to agree with what someone has said, possibly translated, respectively, as "Yes, it is like that" and "Yes, yes, it *is* like that." そうそう in particular, however, has another function, which is to indicate that the speaker has suddenly recalled something—a forgotten errand, task, or incident from the past. The phrase is used both when talking to others and when talking to oneself, as illustrated below.

<u>そうそう</u>、ジムからのメッセージが入ってたよ。電話してって。

Sōsō, Jimu kara no messēji ga haitte 'ta yo. Denwa shite tte.

Oh, yes. You got a voice message from Jim. He said to call.

明日は何をするんだったかな。あ、<u>そうそう</u>、郵便局に行かなきゃいけないんだ。

Ashita wa nani o suru n' datta ka na. A, sōsō, yūbin-kyoku ni ikanakya ikenai n' da.

Now, what was I supposed to do tomorrow? Oh, I know. I'm supposed to go the post office.

そうしてみると

Literally the phrase means "when looked at in that way" and refers back to a previous statement that causes the speaker to see things in a new light or which leads to another thought.

A: きのうのテスト、みんなできなかったんですって。だれもAはとらなかったそうよ。

Kinō no tesuto, minna dekinakatta n' desu tte. Dare mo A wa toranakatta sō yo.

I heard that no one did well on yesterday's test. They say nobody got an A.

B: そうか。<u>そうしてみると</u>、僕のBは、悪くはないんだよな。

Sō ka. Sō shite miru to, boku no B wa, waruku wa nai n' da yo na.

Is that right? In that case, my B is not so bad, is it.

A: 大雪で新幹線が運行停止になったんだって。昔の汽車は雪なんかで止まったりしなかったよね。

Ōyuki de Shinkansen ga unkō-teishi ni natta n' da tte. Mukashi no kisha wa yuki nanka de tomattari shinakatta yo ne.

I heard that the bullet trains were held up due to a heavy snowfall. In the old days trains weren't held up by a little snow, were they.

B: そうだよね。<u>そうしてみると</u>、昔の汽車の方が頑丈だったのかな。

Sō da yo ne. Sō shite miru to, mukashi no kisha no hō ga jōbu datta no ka na.

You're right. Thinking about it, I wonder if trains in the old days were more solidly built.

彼の息子がもう35歳……<u>そうして見ると</u>、彼ももうすぐ還暦というわけか。

Kare no musuko ga mō sanjūgo-sai … sō shite miru to, kare mo mō sugu kanreki to iu wake ka.

His son is already thirty-five.... In that case, he himself must be nearing sixty.

くせ（に）

くせ（に）always implies an emotional reaction or feeling of resentment against the subject on the part of the speaker. When その precedes the phrase, it refers to a previously mentioned or understood matter, statement, or bit of information. Compare the following examples. What the speaker means is the same.

> 彼は、いつも勝手に人のものを使うくせに、自分のもの
> は絶対に貸してくれないんです。
>
> *Kare wa, itsumo katte ni hito no mono o tsukau kuse ni, jibun no mono wa zettai ni kashite kurenai n' desu.*

> 彼は、いつも勝手に人のものを使うんです。そのくせ、
> 自分のものは絶対に貸してくれないんですから。
>
> *Kare wa, itsumo katte ni hito no mono o tsukau n' desu. Sono kuse, jibun no mono wa zettai ni kashite kurenai n' desu kara.*
>
> He always uses other people's things without permission, but he himself never lends you anything of his own.

のに may be used in place of くせに, but くせに is stronger and harsher. When のに directly follows a noun, it becomes なのに, while くせに becomes のくせに.

> ここは静かなのに、眠れない。
>
> *Koko wa shizuka na no ni, nemurenai.*
>
> It's quiet here, but still I can't sleep.

> 浩子は小学生のくせに生意気だから、一緒に出かけたく
> ない。
>
> *Hiroko wa shōgaku-sei no kuse ni namaiki da kara, issho ni dekaketaku nai.*
>
> For an elementary school kid, Hiroko is such a smart aleck that I don't want to take her out with me.

それはそうと

This expression (lit., with that being like that) is used when the speaker tries to change the topic of conversation. While similar in meaning to ところで ("by the way" or "incidentally") it is more commonly used when the topic relates to something shared by the speaker and the listener.

<u>それはそうと</u>、最近ケンを見かけないけど……。
Sore wa sō to, saikin Ken o mikakenai kedo ...
By the way, I haven't seen Ken around recently.

A: <u>それはそうと</u>、京都で、ばったりジョンに会ったんです。
Sore wa sō to, Kyōto de, battari Jon ni atta n' desu.
By the way, I ran into John in Kyoto.

B: 奇遇ね。驚いたでしょう?
Kigū ne. Odoroita deshō?
What a coincidence! A big surprise for you, I bet.

そんな(あ)

そんな literally means "that kind of" and is commonly used in that sense. However, it is also used—probably more commonly by women—to softly protest or complain about something shocking to the speaker that has suddenly surfaced in the course of conversation. Generally it stands on its own as an independent expression, but a full-blown sentence would read something like one of the following, with the ellipses being replaced by such words as ひどい (awful), 意地が悪い (いじがわるい; mean), 薄情な (はくじょうな; coldhearted), or 冷たい (つめたい; cold).

そんなの／ことを言うのは、……です。
Sonna no/koto o iu no wa, ... desu.
It's ... of you to say something like that.

そんな……ことを言わないでください。
Sonna ... koto o iwanai de kudasai.
Please don't say such a ... thing.

Here are some samples in full-sentence form.

A: また授業料が上がるんだって。
Mata jugyō-ryō ga agaru n' da tte.
I heard that they are going to raise the tuition again.

B: <u>そんな</u>!!
Sonna!!
That's terrible!

A: 来月からお小遣いを減らしますからね。五千円ね。
Raigetsu kara okozukai o herashimasu kara ne. Gosen-en ne.
You'll have less spending money from next month. Down to ¥5,000.

B: <u>そんな</u>!! それじゃやっていけないよ。
Sonna!! Sore ja yatte ikenai yo.
You're kidding! I can't get by on that.

それで／で

それで might be literally translated as "with that" and で understood as its truncated form, and they could be paraphrased as "and then" and "and." They serve as short, convenient ways of encouraging the speaker to continue with his or her story.

A: いい人だと思ったからしばらく付き合ってたんだけど、就職して東京に行ってしまって。
Ii hito da to omotta kara shibaraku tsukiatte 'ta n' da kedo, shūshoku shite Tōkyō ni itte shimatte.
I thought he was a nice person, so I was dating for a while, but he found a job and moved to Tokyo, so ...

B: それで？／で？
Sore de?/De?
And then?

A: それっきり。
Sore kkiri.
That's the last I heard from him.

As a conjunctive, それで may also be used in a statement to give a reason, meaning "that's why" or "therefore."

A: きのうは、なぜクラスを休んだんですか。
Kinō wa, naze kurasu o yasunda n' desu ka.
Why didn't you come to class yesterday?

B: すみません。頭ががんがんしてどうしても起きられなかったんです。それで仕方なく、アスピリンを飲んで寝ていたんです。
Sumimasen. Atama ga gangan shite dōshite mo okirarenakatta n' desu. Sore de shikata naku, asupirin o nonde nete ita n' desu.
I'm sorry. I had this pounding headache and simply couldn't get up. So I had no choice but to take some aspirin and stay in bed.

それからというもの（は）

This phrase (lit., the thing after that) is similar in meaning to the everyday conjunction それから ("after that"), but whereas それから focuses on a simple sequence of events, それからというもの（は）indicates that some substantive change has taken place since the point of time in question.

今日は、東京駅で待ち合わせて一緒に食事をした。それから渋谷に映画を見に行った。
Kyō wa, Tōkyō-eki de machiawasete issho ni shokuji o shita. Sore kara Shibuya ni eiga o mi ni itta.
Today we met at Tokyo Station and went to eat together. And then we went to Shibuya to see a movie.

それからというもの、おじいさんは、毎日、黄金の入っ
た竹を見つけるようになった。

*Sore kara to iu mono, ojiisan wa, mainichi, kogane no
haitta take o mitsukeru yō ni natta.*

Everyday since that day (when he found a tiny princess
inside a shiny bamboo tree), the old man began to
find a bamboo tree filled with gold.

それからというもの、彼はまったく車に乗ることをやめ
てしまった。

*Sore kara to iu mono, kara wa mattaku kuruma ni noru
koto o yamete shimatta.*

Since that day, he completely quit driving.

それ以来 may replace それからというもの（は）：

それ以来、彼はまったく車に乗ることをやめてしまった。

*Sore irai, kare wa mattaku kuruma ni noru koto o yamete
shimatta.*

Since then, he has given up driving altogether.

そのそばから……〜ていく／そのそばから……〜て しまう

そば ("nearby," "side") generally shows location, but when
it is followed by から, it indicates that two actions have
occurred one after another. The verb preceding そば is in
the dictionary form.

余程お腹が空いているとみえて、つくるそばから、食べ
てしまう。

*Yohodo onaka ga suite iru to miete, tsukuru soba kara,
tabete shimau.*

He must have been awfully hungry. He ate it up as fast
as I could make it.

When there is some break between the two activities, the
〜た form of a verb is used instead of the dictionary form.

When this happens, 〜たと思ったら ("just as I thought") precedes the phrase and そば is replaced by はし.

やっと工事が済んだと思ったら、<u>済んだはしから</u>又やり直している。

Yatto kōji ga sunda to omottara, sunda hashi kara mata yarinaoshite iru.

Just as I was thinking that they had finally finished the construction work, now they're starting all over again.

タンポポが可愛い花を咲かせたと思ったら、<u>咲かせたはしから</u>子供たちが摘んで行ってしまった。

Tanpopo ga kawaii hana o sakaseta to omottara, sakaseta hashi kara kodomo-tachi ga tsumande itte shimatta.

Just as I was thinking the dandelions had produced such cute little blossoms, some children came right along and picked them all.

When the verb is understood from context or from an immediately preceding statement, その replaces the verb. The phrase そのそば often follows a verb ending in 〜ても ("even if") and precedes such verb endings as 〜てしまう ("completely/unfortunately") or 〜ていく ("keep doing").

せっかく苗を植えても、<u>そのそばから</u>犬が来て堀り返してしまう。

Sekkaku nae o uete mo, sono soba kara inu ga kite hori-kaeshite shimau.

Even though I go to a lot of trouble to plant the seedlings, a dog comes around right after that and digs them up.

ど Words

どちらかといえば

The phrase literally means "if I say which (of the two)" and is used when the speaker has to make a choice between two things. In casual conversation, どっちかといえば can also be used.

A: 週末でもよろしいですか。

Shūmatsu de mo yoroshii desu ka.

Is the weekend convenient for you?

B: ええ。でもどちらかといえば、月曜日の方がいいのですが。

Ee. Demo dochira ka to ieba, getsuyō-bi no hō ga ii no desu ga.

Yes, it is. But if there is a choice in the matter, I would say that Monday would be better for me.

A: マリが来月結婚するのよ。彼って全然ハンサムじゃないんだって。

Mari ga raigetsu kekkon suru no yo. Kare tte, zenzen hansamu ja nai n' da tte.

Mari will get married next month. He is not handsome at all, I heard.

B: 彼女は、<u>どっちかといえば</u>面食いなのにね。よっぽど経済的条件でもよかったのかしら。

Kanojo wa, dotchi ka to ieba menkui na no ni ne. Yoppodo keizai-teki jōken de mo yokatta no kashira.

And, if anything, good looks are what mean most to her. I wonder if it was his financial situation or something that was particularly good.

A: 和食と中華とどっちが好き？

Washoku to chūka to dotchi ga suki?

Which do you like better, Japanese food or Chinese food?

B: そうだね。どっちも好きだけど、<u>どっちかといえば</u>、和食かな。

Sō da ne. Dotchi mo suki da kedo, dotchi ka to ieba, washoku ka na.

Well, yeah. I like both, but if I had to choose, I'd probably say Japanese food.

どこそこ

どこそこ (lit., where-there) refers to an unspecified location

or place and might be translated as "so-and-so" or "such-and-such."

　『どこそこのフランス料理はおいしい』とか『どこそこの
　　店は安い』とか、他愛のない話に花が咲いている。

"Dokosoko no furansu ryōri wa oishii" toka "dokosoko no mise wa yasui" toka, tawai no nai hanashi ni hana ga saite iru.

They are engaged in such small talk as "The French cuisine at such-and-such a restaurant is good" or "Things are cheaper at such-and-such a store."

　世田谷のどこそこに行けとは言うんですけど、どう行く
　　のかは教えてくれないんですよ。

Setagaya no dokosoko ni ike to wa iu n' desu kedo, dō iku no ka wa oshiete kurenai n' desu yo.

He says to go to such-and-such a place in Setagaya, but he won't tell me how to get there.

どこ吹く風

どこ吹く風 (lit., where does the wind blow) is used in reference to someone who could care less about a certain matter, is not interested in hearing about it, and is unaffected by what others say in relation to that matter.

　彼女は、なにを言っても「どこ吹く風」だから、話しても無
　　駄です。

Kanojo wa, nani o itte mo "doko fuku kaze" da kara, hanashite mo muda desu.

It's no use talking to her. No matter what you say, it's like water off a duck's back.

　かな子は、親の言うことなんかどこ吹く風で、遊び歩い
　　ている。

Kanako wa, oya no iu koto nanka doko fuku kaze de, aso-biaruite iru.

Kanako is always out having fun, turning a deaf ear to what her parents say.

どこの馬の骨

どこの馬の骨 (lit., bones of a horse from who knows where) refers to someone whose family background is not clear or who is considered of lower social standing. Needless to say, it is used in a highly derogatory sense. It often appears in the phrase どこの馬の骨だかしらないけれど.

彼は、<u>どこの馬の骨だかも分からない</u>男に可愛い娘をとられたといって、ぶつぶつ言っている。

Kare wa, doko no uma no hone da ka mo wakaranai otoko ni kawaii musume o torareta to itte, butsubutsu itte iru.

He keeps grumbling that he lost his dear daughter to some Joe Blow from who knows where.

A: 隣に移ってきた人、なんなのかしら。偉そうな話し方するけど。

Tonari ni utsutte kita hito, nan na no kashira. Erasō na hanashikata suru kedo.

Who does the man who moved in next door think he is, I wonder. He talks like he was God's gift to humankind.

B: あんなの、<u>どこの馬の骨だかしらないけど</u>、いやな感じ。

Anna no, doko no uma no hone da ka shiranai kedo, iya na kanji.

Oh, that creep. I don't know what woodwork he crawled out of, but he sure puts you off.

どこのどいつ

どいつ is the vulgar equivalent of だれ, or "who," and is mainly used by men. Most often it has derogatory connotations.

大事にしていた壺を割ったりしたのは<u>どこのどいつ</u>だ！？

Daiji ni shite ita tsubo o wattari shita no wa doko no doitsu da!?

Who in the dickens broke my precious vase?

どこのどいつが言ったのかしらないけど、俺がそんなこ
と言うはずないだろう。

*Doko no doitsu ga itta no ka shiranai kedo, ore ga sonna
koto iu hazu nai darō.*

I don't know who on earth told you, but you should
know better than to think I'd say anything like that.

どこからともなく

どこからともなく (lit., from nowhere at all) tells that something or someone suddenly appears or comes out of nowhere. The opposite is どこへともなく, in which the
subject goes away to an uncertain place. In other words,
the former suggests that *from where* is uncertain, while
the latter suggests that *to where* is uncertain.

あの猫は、夕食の支度を始めると、どこからともなく現
れる。

*Ano neko wa, yūshoku no shitaku o hajimeru to, doko
kara to mo naku arawareru.*

Whenever I start preparing supper, that cat appears out
of nowhere.

どこからともなく、沈丁花の甘い香りがただよってくる。

*Doko kara to mo naku, jinchōge no amai kaori ga tada-
yotte kuru.*

Out of nowhere, the sweet fragrance of daphne flowers
comes drifting in the air.

男は、どこへともなく去っていった。

Otoko wa, doko e to mo naku satte itta.

The man went away to who knows where.

放されたツルは、どこへともなく飛んでいった。

Hanasareta tsuru wa, doko e to mo naku tonde itta.

The crane that was set free flew away to who knows
where.

どうにかこうにか／どうやらこうやら

どう means "which way" and こう "this way." They combine as shown above into set phrases meaning "somehow or other." They are interchangeable and indicate that the subject is somehow handling a knotty problem or surviving a difficult situation.

A: 新しい仕事、どう?

Atarashii shigoto, dō?

How's your new job?

B: <u>どうにかこうにか</u>やってます。だんだん慣れてきました。

Dō ni ka kō ni ka yatte 'masu. Dandan narete kimashita.

I'm managing somehow or other. I'm gradually getting used to it.

ペーパーは<u>どうにかこうにか</u>書き上げたけど、まだ試験が三つも残っているから……。

Pēpā wa dō ni ka kō ni ka kakiageta kedo, mada shiken ga mittsu mo nokotte iru kara ...

Somehow I managed to finish my paper, but I still have to take three exams, so ...

不景気な一年だったけど、<u>どうやらこうやら</u>無事新年が迎えられそうだ。

Fu-keiki na ichinen datta kedo, dō yara kō yara buji shin-nen ga mukaeraresō da.

Economic conditions were bad, but somehow or other it seems we'll be able to greet the new year.

<u>どうやらこうやら</u>目的地に行き着いた時には、もう暗くなっていた。

Dō yara kō yara mokuteki-chi ni ikitsuita toki ni wa, mō kuraku natte ita.

When somehow or other we managed to reach our destination, it was already dark.

どこまで

どこまで appears in questions with the meaning "how far." It can be used both literally and figuratively.

A: この高速道路は、<u>どこまで</u>続いているの？

Kono kōsoku-dōro wa, doko made tsuzuite iru no?

How far does this highway go?

B:『東名』っていうんだから名古屋までででしょう。

"Tōmei" tte iu n' da kara Nagoya made deshō.

I think it goes as far as Nagoya since it's called the "Tomei [Tokyo–Nagoya] Highway."

この前借りたお金をまだ返してもいないのに、また借りに来るなんて、<u>どこまで</u>図々しいんだろう。

Kono mae karita okane o mada kaeshite mo inai no ni, mata kari ni kuru nante, doko made zūzūshii n' darō.

Even though he hasn't paid back the money he borrowed the other day, he's come to ask for more! How nervy can you get?

A: あの学生は、ろくに勉強もしないくせに、A をくれなんて言うんですよ。

Ano gakusei wa, roku ni benkyō mo shinai kuse ni, A o kure nante iu n' desu yo.

Even though that student doesn't study worth a darn, she is asking for an A.

B: いつもそうなの。 まったく<u>どこまで</u>厚かましいのか。

Itsumo sō na no. Mattaku doko made atsukamashii no ka.

She's always like that. Really, how pushy can you get?

どこまでも

どこまでも (lit., as far as you can) may be used in reference to actual distance or, figuratively, to mean "all the way."

この道を<u>どこまでも</u>行くと、突き当たりに本屋があります。そこから右に四軒目です。

Kono michi o doko made mo iku to, tsukiatari ni honya ga arimasu. Soko kara migi ni yonken-me desu.

If you go all the way down this street, there is a bookstore at the end. It's the fourth building on the right.

うちの犬は、私が出かけると<u>どこまでも</u>ついて来ようとするんです。

Uchi no inu wa, watashi ga dakakeru to doko made mo tsuite koyō to suru n' desu.

Whenever I go out, my dog tries to follow me as far as she possibly can.

検事側は、<u>どこまでも</u>要求を変えない意向らしい。

Kenji-gawa wa, doko made mo yōkyū o kaenai ikō rashii.

It seems the prosecution has no intention whatsoever of changing their demands.

組合側は、要求が受け入れられなければ、我々は<u>どこまでも</u>闘うと言っている。

Kumiai-gawa wa, yōkyū ga ukeirerarenakereba, wareware wa doko made mo tatakau to itte iru.

In case their demands are not met, the union says they will fight to the very end.

どこまで〜たっけ

っけ is an interrogative ending that indicates the speaker has lost his or her train of thought. The question is addressed either to the speaker him- or herself or to another party. By saying, どこまで〜たっけ, the speaker is in effect saying, "Where was I?"

A: ええっと、<u>どこまでいったっけ</u>？

Ētto, doko made itta kke?

Now, where was I?

B: 横浜のレストランに行ったとこまで。

Yokohama no resutoran ni itta toko made.

You were talking about the restaurant in Yokohama you went to.

どこまでやったっけ? あ、思い出した。ワープロに入れようとしてたんだ。

Doko made yatta kke? A, omoidashita. Wāpuro ni ireyō to shite 'ta n' da.

Now, what was I doing? Ah, now I remember. I was going to put this into the word processer.

Other examples of っけ are:

私、そんなこと言ったっけ?
Watashi, sonna koto itta kke?
Did I say that?

何しにきたんだっけ?
Nani shi ni kita n' da kke?
What did I come to do? / What did I come here for?

あれ、誰だっけ?
Are, dare da kke?
Now, who was that? / Now, what was her name?

どことなく

どことなく might be more or less literally translated as "not anywhere specifically" and has the meaning of "in some vague way." It is very similar to なんとなく ("not anything specifically"), but the former generally indicates that the speaker cannot pinpoint "what or where," whereas the latter does not specify "why or how." Both are used to express impressions concerning feelings or appearances.

A: あの子、<u>どことなく</u>島さんに似てると思わない？

Ano ko, doko to naku Shima-san ni nite 'ru to omowanai?

Doesn't that young man over there remind you somehow of Mr. Shima?

B: あたりまえよ。あの子、島さんの息子さんだもの。

Atarimae yo. Ano ko, Shima-san no musuko-san da mono.

Of course he does. After all, he's Mr. Shima's son.

<u>どことなく</u>寂れた感じのこの町が、かつて宿場としてに
ぎわっていたとは。

*Doko to naku sabireta kanji no kono machi ga, katsute
shukuba toshite nigiwatte ita to wa.*

To think that this desolate-looking place was once a
prosperous and lively post town.

あの子、美人じゃないけど、<u>なんとなく</u>愛嬌があって可
愛いので人気がある。

*Ano ko, bijin ja nai kedo, nan to naku aikyō ga atte kawaii
no de ninki ga aru.*

She is not beautiful, but she's popular because she's
cute and there's something charming about her.

今日は、<u>なんとなく</u>疲れちゃった。どうしてかな。

Kyō wa, nan to naku tsukarechatta. Dōshite ka na.

I don't know why, but I feel tired today.

どうしようもない

しようがない literally means "there is no way," but as a set
phrase it means "cannot be helped" or "there is no other
choice." It often indicates a feeling of regret, disappointment, or frustration. When どう precedes the phrase, the
particle が changes to も, and the phrase becomes a more
emphatic representation of the speaker's feelings. To add a
feeling of being too late or overdue, add もう to the beginning

of the phrase. どうしようもない may be replaced by どうにもならない with little change in meaning.

迎えに来てもらえなかったら、タクシーで行くより<u>仕方がない／しようがない</u>。

Mukae ni kite moraenakattara, takushī de iku yori shikata ga nai/shiyō ga nai.

If no one comes to pick me up, I'll have no choice but to take a taxi.

<u>しようがない</u>人ねえ。

Shiyō ga nai hito nee.

You're a hopeless case. / What am I going to do with you?

A: C なんてひどい。B はくれると思っていたのに。

C nante hidoi. B wa kureru to omotte ita no ni.

A C! How awful. I thought I'd get a B.

B: <u>しようがない／しかたがない</u>でしょ。自分がサボってたんだから。

Shiyō ga nai/shikata ga nai desho. Jibun ga sabotte 'ta n' da kara.

It can't be help. You were the one who was goofing off.

この土砂降りじゃ<u>どうしようもない</u>よ。今日は行くのやめよう。

Kono doshaburi ja dō shiyō mo nai yo. Kyō wa iku no yameyō.

It's hopeless in this kind of heavy rain. Let's give up going today.

今となっては、<u>もうどうしようもない／どうにもならない</u>よ。いい加減あきらめよう。

Ima to natte wa, mō dō shiyō mo nai/dō ni mo naranai yo. Iikagen akirameyō.

It's too late to do anything about it now. Let's just forget about it.

どうにも

When どうにも is used with a negative ending, it indicates that nothing can be done to resolve a situation. When it precedes a descriptive word, the ending verb is not negative but the overall connotation is; see the last example below.

> <u>どうにもならない</u>ことに、いつまでもくよくよしていないで。元気だしなさいよ。
>
> *Dō ni mo naranai koto ni, itsu made mo kuyokuyo shite inai de. Genki dashinasai yo.*
>
> Don't be continually fretting over things you can't do anything about. Cheer up.

> A: あれ、どうにかならないのかしら?
>
> *Are, dō ni ka naranai no kashira.*
>
> Can't they do something about that?

> B: 言ってみたんだけど、<u>どうにもならない</u>んだっていうのよ。
>
> *Itte mita n' da kedo, dō ni mo naranai n' da tte iu no yo.*
>
> I mentioned it, but they said nothing could be done.

> この辺の家が欲しいと思ったけど、<u>どうにも</u>高いのであきらめた。
>
> *Kono hen no ie ga hoshii to omotta kedo, dō ni mo takai no de akirameta.*
>
> I wanted to buy a house in this area, but they're so awfully expensive I gave up.

どうかすると

どうかすると refers to both possibilities and tendencies. In the first sense, it is often followed by ～可能性がある and ～かねない; in the second sense ～がちだ. ややもすると or ややもすれば can be used in the same way, but only when indicating a tendency, not a possibility.

このような紛争は、<u>どうかすると</u>大きな社会問題にまで
発展<u>しかねない</u>。

*Kono yō na funsō wa, dō ka suru to ōkina shakai mondai
ni made hatten shikanenai.*

A dispute of this kind could possibly develop into a serious social problem.

快復に向かってはいるが、<u>どうかすると</u>まだ肺炎を併発
する<u>可能性がある</u>と、医者に言われた。

*Kaifuku ni mukatte wa iru ga, dō ka suru to mada haien
o heihatsu suru kanō-sei ga aru to, isha ni iwareta.*

The doctor said that although she was getting better,
there was the possibility of it developing into pneu-
monia.

彼女は、最近、<u>どうかすると</u> ふさぎ<u>がち</u>になる。

Kanojo wa, saikin, dō ka suru to fusagigachi ni naru.

Recently she tends to become depressed.

この腕時計は、<u>ややもすると</u> 遅れ<u>がち</u>なんです。

Kono ude-dokei wa, yaya mo suru to okuregachi nan desu.

This watch tends to be slow.

な Words

While な words do not belong to the こそあど group, there
are a number of interesting phrases that should be noted.
な words usually appear as interrogatives, such as なに
("what") and なぜ ("why"). Among the な words, the most
commonly used in set phrases is なに.

なにがなんでも

なにがなんでも is used to intensify the following statement, such as a strong intention or an expression of deter-
mination. It may be used interchangeably with なにがあろ
うと.

いったん始めたら、<u>なにがなんでも</u>やり通すべきです。

Ittan hajimetara, nani ga nan de mo yaritōsu beki desu.

Once started, you should carry through at any cost.

欲しいと思ったものは<u>なにがなんでも</u>手に入れるという
のがミカの主義らしいです。

*Hoshii to omotta mono wa nani ga nan de mo te ni ireru
to iu no ga Mika no shugi rashii desu.*

It seems that Mika's philosophy of life is to get whatever she wants, no matter what.

<u>何があろうと</u>、必ずまた会いに来ます。

Nani ga arō to, kanarazu mata ai ni kimasu.

No matter what happens, I'll definitely come to see you
once again.

なにからなにまで

This phrase means "from A to Z," covering everything. It
is often used in regard to gratitude or appreciation.

あの方には、<u>なにからなにまで</u>お世話になり、大変感謝
しております。

*Ano kata ni wa, nani kara nani made osewa ni nari, tai-
hen kansha shite orimasu.*

She took care of everything for me. I appreciate it very
much.

<u>なにからなにまで</u>人にやらせておいて、礼も言わない。

Nani kara nani made hito ni yarasete oite, rei mo iwanai.

He has me/you do everything for him but never says a
word of thanks.

なにもかも

なにもかも also means "everything," but it often has negative connotations. The difference between なにからなに

まで (discussed immediately above) and なにもかも is that the former looks at the whole in terms of individual units whereas the latter refers to the entire entity.

これでなにもかも終わりです。また一からやり直さなければ。

Kore de nanimo kamo owari desu. Mata ichi kara yari-naosanakereba.

It's all over now. I've got to start all over again from scratch.

いっぺんになにもかもやれって言っても無理ですよ。

Ippen ni nanimo kamo yare tte itte mo muri desu yo.

It's impossible to do everything at once, no matter what you say.

なにもかもいやになった。こんな仕事、もう辞めたいよ。

Nanimo kamo iya ni natta. Konna shigoto, mō yametai yo.

I'm sick and tired of everything. I've had more than enough of this kind of work.

何気なく／何気ない

何気（なにげ）なく／何気ない (lit., no intention whatsoever) indicates that something was done in a very casual manner or unintentionally. Sometimes it refers to a pretense.

彼は、何気ない口調で「結婚しよう」と言った。

Kara wa, nanige nai kuchō de "kekkon shiyō" to itta.

In a casual tone, he said, "Let's get married."

犯人は、隣人を装い何気ない素振りで被害者に話しかけてきたという。

Hannin wa, rinjin o yosooi nanige nai soburi de higaisha ni hanashikakete kita to iu.

They say that the criminal pretended to be a neighbor and casually came up to speak to the victim.

何気なく外をみると、いつの間にか雪になっていた。

Nanige naku soto o miru to, itsu no ma ni ka yuki ni natte ita.

When I happened to look outside, I saw it had started to snow.

何が何だか

何が何だか (lit., what is what?) suggests that the speaker is puzzled or confused. It always has a negative connotation.

動転していたので、何が何だか判断する力さえ失っていた。

Dōten shite ita no de, nani ga nan da ka handan suru chikara sae ushinatte ita.

Upset and confused, I didn't know which end was up and couldn't make a decision.

あんまり問題が複雑で、何が何だかわからなくなってしまった。

Anmari mondai ga fukuzatsu de, nani ga nan da ka wakaranaku natte shimatta.

The problem was so complicated that I couldn't tell what was what anymore.

何より

何（なに）より indicates that something is a superlative example of its kind. It is also used in greetings to show that the speaker is pleased about some news or a situation.

私が何より（も）嫌いなのは、ゴキブリです。

Watashi ga nani yori (mo) kirai na no wa, gokiburi desu.

What I hate most are cockroaches.

A: 何もありませんが……。

Nani mo arimasen ga …

I'm sorry that I don't have anything special to offer.

B: いえ、私には家庭料理が<u>何より</u>のごちそうです。

Ie, watashi ni wa katei-ryōri ga nani yori no gochisō desu.

Don't concern yourself about that. I love homemade cooking more than anything.

元気で活躍なさっていらっしゃるとのこと、<u>何より</u>です。

Genki de katsuyaku nasatte irassharu to no koto, nani yori desu.

I am happy to hear that you have been in good health and are as active as ever.

何分

何分 (なにぶん), literally meaning "whatever degree," is used in two ways. One is to replace どうぞ in a request. In this case, the equally formal 何卒 (なにとぞ) may replace 何分. In the second usage of 何分, it may be used in explanation or excuse, meaning "after all" or "in any case." 何せ may also be used in this sense.

お忙しいところ申し訳ありませんが、<u>何分／何卒</u>よろしくお願い申し上げます。

Oisogashii tokoro mōshiwake arimasen ga, nanibun/nanitozo yoroshiku onegai mōshiagemasu.

I realize that you are terribly busy, but I would really appreciate your help.

行き届かないところもあったかと思いますが、<u>何分／何せ</u>まだ見習い中なもので、今回のことは、お許しください。

Yukitodokanai tokoro mo atta ka to omoimasu ga, nani-bun/nanise mada minarai-chū na mono de, konkai no koto wa, oyurushi kudasai.

His service may have been unsatisfactory, but in any case he is still a trainee, so please bear with us this once.

なにかにつけ／なにくれとなく

なにかにつけ (lit., concerning something or other) and なにくれとなく (without this or that) are used in similar ways, both meaning "various" or "sundry." However, whereas the former has both positive and negative usages, the latter seems to be used mostly in a positive sense.

母は、<u>なにかにつけ</u>愚痴を言う。

Haha wa, nani ka ni tsuke guchi o iu.

My mother complains about all kinds of things.

あの人は、今でも<u>なにかにつけ</u>便りをくれます。

Ano hito wa, ima de mo nani ka ni tsuke tayori o kuremasu.

Even now he still writes on various occasions.

先輩や同僚が、<u>なにくれとなく</u>助けてくれるので仕事がしやすいです。

Senpai ya dōryō ga, nani kure to naku tasukete kureru no de shigoto ga shiyasui desu.

People senior to me and my other colleagues help me in various ways, making my work much easier.

なにやかや（と）

なにやかや（と）is used to list indefinite things, like English "this and that" or "one thing and another."

<u>なにやかや</u>と雑用に追われていたもので、返事が遅れてしまいました。

Naniya kaya to zatsuyō ni owarete ita mono de, henji ga okurete shimaimashita.

Unfortunately, with all kinds of busy work coming up, I was unable to respond (to your letter) immediately.

<u>なにやかや</u>と買っているうちに、五百ドルも使ってしまった。

Naniya kaya to katte iru uchi ni, gohyaku-doru mo tsukatte shimatta.

What with buying this and that, I ended up spending all of $500.

❷

IDIOMATIC EXPRESSIONS

Part 2 deals with idiomatic expressions that, on the whole, are not properly explained in textbooks and dictionaries, or are presented in such simple forms that the student remains unprepared for more complicated instances. By definition, idiomatic expressions cannot be understood literally or in a grammatically orthodox manner. Over time they have acquired particular characteristics that must be studied on their own. Here, we discuss and exemplify idiomatic expressions that are commonly found in intermediate textbooks and Japanese language proficiency tests.

いつの間にか

This expression (lit., at whatever time) indicates that something has occurred without the speaker noticing or realizing it. It is often used in a statement about habitual or general phenomena, as seen in the first example below. The ～た form of the verb (indicating past or perfective tense) may occur with ようだ, らしい, or とみえる ("It seems that") when the statement is conjectural.

> あの猫は、夕食時になると、<u>いつの間にか</u>どこからか<u>現れる</u>んですよ。
>
> *Ano neko wa, yūshoku-doki ni naru to, itsu no ma ni ka doko kara ka arawareru n' desu yo.*

Without your realizing it, the cat appears out of nowhere around dinnertime.

外は、<u>いつの間にか</u>、雪になった<u>ようだ</u>。

Soto wa, itsu no ma ni ka, yuki ni natta yō da.

It seemed to have started snowing outside without my realizing it.

<u>いつの間にか</u>、列車の網棚に置いてあった鞄がなくなっていた。

Itsu no ma ni ka, ressha no amidana ni oite atta kaban ga nakunatte ita.

Without my realizing it, the bag I had put up on the train rack had disappeared.

～たばかりに……～てしまった／～たばかりに……～ざるを得なくなった

～たばかりに indicates the sole reason for an adverse result. It is often used in combination with verb endings like ～てしまった, which express the speaker's regret, or the set phrase ～ざるを得ない ("cannot help but do.")

上司にたてついた<u>たばかりに</u>、彼は会社を辞め<u>ざるを得な</u><u>くなった</u>。

Jōshi ni tatetsuita bakari ni, kare wa kaisha o yamezaru o enaku natta.

For the simple reason that he stood up to his boss, he finally had no choice but to quit the company.

なまじ ("carelessly," "thoughtlessly," or "halfway") may be added as an intensifier. なまじっか is a colloquial variation.

<u>なまじ</u>金持ちになった<u>たばかりに</u>、ジョンの人生は孤独なものとなっ<u>てしまった</u>。

Namaji kanemochi ni natta bakari ni, Jon no jinsei wa kodoku na mono to natte shimatta.

For the simple reason that John became wealthy, his life turned out to be a lonely one.

なまじっか今日は給料日だなんて口にしたばかりにおご
らせられちゃった／おごらされちゃった。

*Namajikka kyō wa kyūryō-bi da nante kuchi ni shita
bakari ni ogoraserarechatta/ogorasarechatta.*

Just because I carelessly mentioned that today was pay-
day, I had to treat everyone.

下手（を）すると

下手（を）すると (lit., if you do it unskillfully) suggests a worst
case scenario. The statement that follows shows the possible undesirable outcome.

下手をすると、快復するまでに一ヵ月はかかるだろうと、
医者に言われた。

*Heta o suru to, kaifuku suru made ni ikkagetsu wa ka-
karu darō to, isha ni iwareta.*

I was told by my doctor that, if worse comes to worst, it
could take a month before I fully recover.

A: この試験の成績、見て。

Kono shiken no seiseki, mite.

Look at these test results.

B: 悪いですねえ。下手すると、高校生より悪いかもしれ
ませんよ。

*Warui desu nē. Heta suru to, kōkō-sei yori warui kamo
shiremasen yo.*

That's bad, isn't it. It's so bad that even a high school
student might do better.

（この雪だと）、下手すると今夜は帰れないかもしれない。

*(Kono yuki da to), heta suru to konya wa kaerenai kamo
shirenai.*

(With this snow) I may not be able to get home tonight,
if worse comes to worst.

せめて

せめて ("at least") expresses the speaker's minimal or least expectation. 〜たい (want to), (〜て)ほしい (want something from someone else), or 〜れば／たらいいのに (why don't you … ／you should …) may follow.

A: お金があったら、世界旅行するんだけどな。

Okane ga attara, sekai-ryokō suru n' da kedo na.

I'd make a trip around the world if I had the money.

B: 私は<u>せめて</u>一生に一度、海外に行ってみ<u>たい</u>。

Watashi wa semete isshō ni ichido, kaigai ni itte mitai.

I'd like to go abroad at least once in my life.

これだけ一生懸命勉強しているんだから、<u>せめて</u>Bはつけ<u>てほしい</u>んだけど……。

Kore dake isshō-kenmei benkyō shite iru n' da kara, semete B wa tsukete hoshii n' da kedo.

Since I'm studying this hard, I hope the teacher will at least give me a B.

<u>せめて</u>、理由ぐらい言ってや<u>れば</u>よかった<u>のに</u>。

Semete, riyū gurai itte yareba yokatta no ni.

You should have at least told her the reason.

〜ては

The basic function of 〜て is to connect verb phrases (see also Shoji, pp. 44–66). When 〜て is followed by は, it has the following functions. First, it may be translated as "if":

<u>行っては</u>いけない。

Itte wa ikenai.

You shouldn't go. (Lit., If you go, things won't turn out well.)

今さらそんなことを<u>言っては</u>、困ります。

Ima sara sonna koto o itte wa, komarimasu.

It's a little late to be saying something like that. (Lit., If you say such a thing at this time, it may cause a problem.)

It describes a repeated occurrence:

あの子は、いたずらを<u>しては</u>先生を怒らせている。

Ano ko wa, itazura o shite wa sensei o okorasete iru.

That child keeps getting into mischief and making the teacher angry.

落ち葉が、風に<u>吹かれては</u>舞い上がった。

Ochiba ga, kaze ni fukarete wa maiagatta.

Fallen leaves kept dancing in the wind. (Lit., Everytime the wind blew, fallen leaves flew up in the air.)

Compare:

落ち葉が、風に<u>吹かれて</u>舞い上がった。

Ochiba ga, kaze ni fukarete maiagatta.

The wind blew, and fallen leaves flew up into the air.

These two sentences look alike, but they are not necessarily the same. 〜ては in the first sentence describes a repetitive occurrence, while 〜て in the second sentence is a one-time occurrence. Thus, 〜ては has two functions: one, to show cause and two, through the addition of は, to show repetition.

It is important to note that because 〜て has other connective functions, its use to indicate cause is somewhat limited (see Shoji pp. 46–48). The relationship of cause and effect has to be fairly clear from context for 〜て to function in this capacity. For example, look at these two sentences.

彼女が<u>病気になって</u>、<u>お見舞に行く</u>んです。

Kanojo ga byōki ni natte, omimai ni iku n' desu.

She got sick, and I am going to visit her.

雨が降って、行けなかったんです。

Ame ga futte, ikenakatta n' desu.

Due to the rain, I couldn't go.

The first sentence sounds awkward because the relationship between the two events is not clear enough (though clear enough from a strictly logical point of view). In the second sentence, even though it has the same grammatical structure as the first, the relationship of cause and effect is perfectly clear. The first sentence can be made acceptable by changing it in either of the following ways:

彼女が病気になって、お見舞いに行くことになりました。
彼女が病気になったので、お見舞いに行くんです。

The point here is that 〜て should not be used to indicate cause unless it is absolutely clear (not just in the speaker's mind) that the relationship between the two clauses is one of cause and effect.

あのう

あのう is a filler used when the proper word refuses to come to mind, the speaker is hesitant, or the speaker is attempting to draw someone's attention.

あのう……ご迷惑でなければ、私も一緒に行かせていただけませんか。

Anō … gomeiwaku de nakereba, watashi mo issho ni ikasete itadakemasen ka.

Excuse me … if it's not a bother, would you mind if I went along with you?

あのう、すみませんが、田中さんのオフィスはどちらでしょうか。

Anō, sumimasen ga, Tanaka-san no ofisu wa dochira deshō ka.

Ah, excuse me, but could you tell me where Mr. Tanaka's office is?

あのう、ここ、空いていますか。

Anō, koko, aite imasu ka.

Excuse me … is this seat taken?

せいぜい

せいぜい ("at most") indicates the speaker's maximum expectations or the limit or range of something, such as price, amount, or ability. It is commonly used with endings such as X までだ (X is the limit), 〜ば／〜たらいいほうだ (it's impossible to expect any more than X), and X ぐらいだ／ぐらいのものだ (what can be expected is just about X). This expression often follows the adverbial phrase 〜ても (even if).

遠いといっても、せいぜい三十分もあれば行けます。

Tōi to itte mo, seizei sanjuppun mo areba ikemasu.

You may think it's far, but you can get there in thirty minutes at most.

高くても、せいぜい五千円ぐらいでしょう。

Takakute mo, seizei gosen-en gurai deshō.

Even if expensive, it'll be about ¥5,000 at most.

せいぜい一年に一度会えれば、いいほうなんです。

Seizei ichinen ni ichido aereba, ii hō nan desu.

If we can see each other even once a year, we are not doing bad.

あの学生にできるのは、せいぜいこれぐらいだと思う。

Ano gakusei ni dekiru no wa, seizei kore gurai da to omou.

I think this is about the best that student can do.

せいぜい is sometimes used in expressions of goodwill, meaning "as much as possible" or "if nothing else."

せいぜい旅行をお楽しみください。

Seizei ryokō o otanoshimi kudasai.

Enjoy your trip as much as possible.

少なくても／少なくとも

Both 少なくても and 少なくとも ("at least") express the speaker's least expectation, estimate, or a condition. 少なくても is a little more colloquial than 少なくとも.

<u>少なくとも</u>一時間十ドルは払ってもらえるだろう。

Sukunaku tomo ichijikan jūdoru wa haratte moraeru darō.

They will probably pay me $10 per hour at least.

忙しいのはわかるけど、<u>少なくても</u>うちに電話ぐらいは
すべきだ。

Isogashii no wa wakaru kedo, sukunakute mo uchi ni den-wa gurai wa subeki da.

I know you're busy, but you should at least call home.

ますます／どんどん

どんどん refers to an action, movement, or phenomenon that is carried out energetically or with notable progress. For instance, the sentence 彼女（かのじょ）はどんどん歩（ある）いて行った means "she kept walking on at a steady pace." This is different from 速（はや）く歩く, where the focus in only on speed. ますます, on the other hand, suggests an increase or acceleration in some quality (e.g., speed, tendency, force, degree) in relation to some previously metioned or inferred point. For example, 成長（せいちょう）して、彼女（かのじょ）はますますきれいになった ("Growing up, she has gotten prettier and prettier") suggests that she was pretty even as a child.

意見があったら、<u>どんどん</u>言ってください。

Iken ga attara, dondon itte kudasai.

If you have any comments, please speak up without hesitation/freely.

川の水がどんどん増えてきている。

Kawa no mizu ga dondon fuete kite iru.

The water in the river keeps on increasing.

おいしいですか。よかった。どんどん食べてくださいね。

Oishii desu ka. Yokatta. Dondon tabete kudasai ne.

Oh, you like it? Good! Please eat as much as you like.

どんどん歩かないと、電車に間に合わないよ。

Dondon arukanai to, densha ni ma ni awanai yo.

If we don't keep walking at a steady pace, we'll miss the train.

トムは、日本女性と結婚して、ますます日本語が上達した。

Tomu wa, Nihon josei to kekkon shite, masumasu Nihongo ga jōtatsu shita.

Since Tom married a Japanese woman, his Japanese has gotten better and better.

ソニアは、ますますお母さんに似てきましたね。

Sonia wa, masumasu okāsan ni nite kimashita ne.

Sonia looks more and more like her mother.

いくら～からって／いくら～からといって

This phrase, which might be paraphrased as "Just because it's …," presents the object that is to be criticized in the rest of the sentence, usually by suggesting that the matter or person in question is excessive or has gone to extremes. It is often followed by a verb such as すぎる (to be excessive, to be too much).

いくらブランド品だからって、これは高すぎます。

Ikura burando-hin da kara tte, kore wa takasugimasu.

Even though it's a brand name, it's still too expensive.

いくら上司だからといって、少し横暴すぎるんじゃない？

Ikura jōshi da kara to itte, sukoshi ōbō sugiru n' ja nai?

Even though he's our boss, he's too high-handed, don't
you think?

In an understood context, いくらなんだって or なんぼなん
だって may be used interchangeably in conversation, but
not in serious writing.

なんぼなんだって、高すぎるよ。

Nanbo nan da tte, takasugiru yo.

No matter what anybody says, it's too expensive.

と言えないことはない／と言えないこともない

This expression, which might be roughly translated as "it is
not impossible to say that," is used to acknowledge another's
opinion but, at the same time, to deny it partially by intro-
ducing a new and contrary factor. The statement before と
is understood from context, and そう ("that") may replace
と.

A: 絶対に有罪だね。無罪になる余地はないよ。

Zettai ni yūzai da ne. Muzai ni naru yochi wa nai yo.

I am sure he's guilty. There is no chance he'll be ac-
quitted.

B: まあ、そう／と言えないこともないけど、彼はいい弁
護士が雇えるから……どうかしらねえ。

*Mā, sō/to ienai koto mo nai kedo, kare wa ii bengo-shi ga
yatoeru kara ... dō kashira nē.*

Well, you could say that, but he can hire a good lawyer,
so I wonder …

A: あそこの料理、どうだった？　期待通り？

Asoko no ryōri, dō datta? Kitai dōri?

How was the food there? As good as you expected?

B: まあ、料理は<u>そう言えないこともないけど</u>、ちょっと
時間がかかりすぎると思うよ。

*Mā, ryōri wa sō ienai koto mo nai kedo, chotto jikan ga
kakarisugiru to omou yo.*

Well, I think you could say that, but they do take a little
too long.

が／は

The particles が and は display subtle differences in usage.
As a general rule, が marks the subject of the immediately
following verb; if there is only one verb in the sentence, of
course が marks the subject of that verb. However, if が
marks the subject of a verb in a subordinate sentence, the
subject of the main verb will be either specified or understood from context, but will not be that marked by が (see
the discussion of commas below for an exception to the
rule). The following sentence shows an example in which
が marks the subject of the subordinate sentence; the subject of the main sentence is understood from context and
is different from that marked by が. (See Shoji, pp. 24–34,
for more on は and が.)

<u>私が</u>もう<u>買った</u>からいいです。

Watashi ga mō katta kara ii desu.

I already bought it, so (understood subject) doesn't need it.

Using this same sentence but substituting は for が, we
get a slightly different situation. は marks the subject-topic
of the main verb (that of the main sentence), but the subject of the verb in the subordinate sentence is determined
by context; it can be the same as that in the main sentence, but it may also be different.

<u>私は</u>もう買ったから<u>いいです</u>。

Watashi wa mō katta kara ii desu.

("I" or understood subject) already bought it, so I don't
need it.

Here are two more contrasting examples with が and は.

私がこの間来た時買いました。

Watashi ga kono aida kita toki kaimashita.

(Understood subject) bought it when I came here the other day.

私はこの間来た時買いました。

Watashi wa kono aida kita toki kaimashita.

I bought it when ("I" or understood subject) came here the other day.

The following two sentences are grammatically the same as the ones above, but there is a logical difference in the sentence containing は. As with the above, it is grammatically possible for the noun marked by は to be the subject-topic of both verbs in the sentence, but since it is logically impossible for 私 to "come here" but also "not be here," the subject of the main sentence must be someone else, who is understood from context. This is an example of where logic takes precedence over grammar.

私がこの間来た時いませんでした。

Watashi ga kono aida kita toki imasen deshita.

When I came the other day, (understood subject) was not here.

私はこの間来た時いませんでした。

Watashi wa kono aida kita toki imasen deshita.

When (understood subject) came the other day, I was not here.

Usually the role of punctuation in Japanese is not as significant as in English, but when the subject marker が is followed by a comma, the comma is important in that it indicates that the noun marked by が is the subject of the main verb of the sentence and possibly also the verb in the subordinate sentence. It should be noted, however, that not all writers follow this convention, so that it is possible that sentences without a comma after が should actually be read as if a comma were present.

私が、この間来た時買いました。

Watashi ga, kono aida kita toki kaimashita.

I (am the one who) bought it when ("I" or understood subject) came the other day.

There are other cases when the presence of a comma is important: for instance, after a noun-modifying clause the comma indicates that it is not to modify the following noun but the one after that. In the sentence below, the comma indicates that 八月に開催される modifies not the immediately following 今回, but rather オリンピック.

八月に開催される、今回のオリンピック

hachigatsu ni kaisai sareru, konkai no orinpikku

this coming Olympics that is to be held in August

の

Identifying the grammatical roles of の is of vital importance. の does not always mean "of," though this is, of course, one of it more common meanings. Here are some tips about the usage of の. (See Shoji, pp. 19–24, for more on this topic.)

1. Common noun   Proper name/pronoun
       A   の   B

A and B are in apposition (i.e., explanatory equivalents) or A is modifying B.

医者のジムさん

  A   B

isha no Jimu-san

Jim, a doctor. Or, Jim who is a doctor.

2. Dictionary form of verb + の (see also #4, below)

Here, の is a nominalizer. In other words, の makes the verb into a noun like an English gerund (… ing) or infinitive (to …).

行くのはいやだ。
Iku no wa iya da.
I hate to go.

3. Noun の Verb + Noun

の immediately followed by a verb marks the subject. In other words, it has the same function as the subject marker が. Note that adjectives and adjectival nouns (e.g., おいしい、きれい) function in the same manner as verbs in this respect.

私の 買った車
Aの　 V　 N
watashi no katta kuruma
the car that I bought

夕日 のきれいな浜辺
　N　 の　Adj　 N
yūhi no kirei na hamabe
a beach where the sunset is beautiful

コーヒーのおいしい店
　 N　 の　Adj　 N
kōhi no oishii mise
a coffee shop where the coffee is good

4. ～のは、～です。
　 A　　 B

In an A-is-B type sentence, when B is a noun, の functions

as a pronominal, and の is defined by B. When B is a descriptive word, の functions as a nominalizer of the preceding verb.

日本に行く<u>の</u>は<u>ジョン</u>です。
    pronom.は   B   です.

Nihon ni iku no wa Jon desu.

The one going to Japan is John. (John is the one going to Japan.)

日本に行く<u>の</u>は、<u>来週</u>です。

Nihon ni iku no wa, raishū desu.

The time when I go to Japan is next week. (I go to Japan next week.)

日本に行く<u>の</u>は<u>いや</u>です。

Nihon ni iku no wa iya desu.

I don't want to go to Japan. (Lit., Going to Japan is not desirable.)

これだけの漢字を一日で覚える<u>の</u>は、<u>無理</u>です。

Kore dake no kanji o ichinichi de oboeru no wa, muri desu.

It is impossible to memorize this many kanji in one day.

In the first sentence above, B is ジョン, so の is a pronominal and replaces 人 (person), while in the second sentence, の replaces 時 (time) because B, 来週, is a time word.

5. ～のです。

The usage of のです (or its variations, んです, のだ, んだ, or simply の) as discussed here changes the tone of a sentence from a direct statement to an explanation or an attempt to persuade. All of these forms occur at the end of a main or subordinate sentence.

すみません。来るつもりだった<u>のです</u>けれど、風邪をひ
いて寝込んでしまったものですから。

> *Sumimasen. Kuru tsumori datta no desu keredo, kaze o hiite nekonde shimatta mono desu kara.*
>
> I'm so sorry. I was planning to come, but I caught a cold and had to stay in bed.

Or, less formally:

> ごめん。来るつもりだった<u>ん</u>だけど、風邪をひいて寝込んでしまった<u>の</u>。
>
> *Gomen. Kuru tsumori datta n' da kedo, kaze o hiite nekonde shimatta no.*
>
> I'm sorry. I was expecting to come, but I caught a cold and ended up in bed.

のです, in the form of ので, can also be used at the end of a clause to offer an explanation for what is to follow in the rest of the sentence. Be careful to note the difference between から, which offers a direct reason, and ので, which offers an explanation. In situations like those represented by the two examples below, either word could be used, although ので would be softer and more indirect.

> 今晩は宿題がたくさんある<u>ので</u>、早く帰らないといけません。
>
> *Konban wa shukudai ga takusan aru no de, hayaku kaeranai to ikemasen.*
>
> I have a lot of homework tonight, so I have to go home early.

> すみません。勉強中に停電になった<u>ので</u>、宿題が半分しかできませんでした。
>
> *Sumimasen. Benkyō-chū ni teiden ni natta no de, shukudai ga hanbun shika dekimasen deshita.*
>
> I'm sorry, but right in the middle of my homework we had a power failure, so I could only get half of it done.

When making requests, however, and offering a reason for the request, から is not likely to be used because it lays stress on one's own, egocentric needs and reasons. Thus the following example would not be acceptable, even though it contains an explanatory の.

交換留学生プログラムに申し込みたい<u>の／んですから</u>、推薦状を書いていただけませんか。

Kōkan-ryūgakusei puroguramu ni mōshikomitai no/n' desu kara, suisen-jō o kaite itadakemasen ka.

Since I'd like to apply for the student exchange program, could you possibly write me a letter of recommendation?

In the above sentence, ので would be much better than から, but given the fact that で is still pointing to one's own reasons, it is not perfect. の／んですが or んだけど would be the best solution since they contain the explanatory の as well as が and けど, which simply connect the two clauses without pointing overtly to a personal reason for the request. The following two examples show this in practice, the first being a rewording of the example above.

交換留学生プログラムに申し込みたい<u>の／んですが</u>、推薦状を書いていただけませんか。

Kōkan-ryūgakusei puroguramu ni mōshikomitai no/n' desu ga, suisen-jō o kaite itadakemasen ka.

I would like to apply for the student exchange program, and I was wondering if you could write a letter of recommendation for me.

郵便局まで行きたい<u>ん</u>だけど、乗せて行ってくれない？

Yūbin-kyoku made ikitai n' da kedo, nosete itte kurenai?

I'd like to go the post office. Could you give me a ride?

かねない

かねない indicates the possibility of something happening. It is preceded by a pre-ます form (e.g., <u>し</u>かねない、<u>なり</u>かねない). It is negative in connotation, suggesting that something undesirable may happen in the future. In other words, this expression indicates feelings of mistrust, worry, or concern on the part of the speaker.

今何とかしなければ、最悪の状態にも<u>なりかねない</u>。

Ima nan to ka shinakereba, saiaku no jōtai ni mo narika-nenai.

Unless we do something now, the situation may deteriorate disasterously.

A: あの学生は、よくカンニングするんですよ。

Ano gakusei wa, yoku kanningu suru n' desu yo.

That student often cheats on his tests.

B: 今度もまた<u>しかねない</u>から、気をつけて。

Kondo mo mata shikanenai kara, ki o tsukete.

He might do it again this time, so keep an eye on him.

かねない and おそれがある (lit., there is a fear that) may be used interchangeably, though the latter is more formal. おそれがある is preceded by the dictionary form instead of a pre-ます form.

最悪の状態に<u>なる</u>おそれがある。

Saiaku no jōtai ni naru osore ga aru.

また<u>する</u>おそれがある。

Mata suru osore ga aru.

というこ と(は)

というこ と (lit., which is to say) is used at the end of sentences in two ways: one, to indicate hearsay, meaning that the speaker is passing on information learned from a third party; and two, in explanation, clarifying or restating what has been stated earlier.

夕べ、富士山に初雪が降った<u>というこ と</u>です。

Yūbe , Fuji-san ni hatsuyuki ga futta to iu koto desu.

They say that the first snow (of the year) fell on Mt. Fuji last night.

A: すみません。明日は急用ができて来られないんですが。

Sumimasen. Ashita wa kyūyō ga dekite korarenai n' desu ga.

I'm sorry, but some urgent business has come up, so I won't be able to come tomorrow.

B: あした試験を受けられない<u>ということ</u>ですか。

Ashita shiken o ukerarenai to iu koto desu ka.

Does that mean you won't be able to take the test tomorrow?

In its explanatory or clarifying sense, ということ may appear at the beginning of a sentence. The following may be used instead of B in the sample dialogue immediately above.

<u>ということ</u>は、あした試験を受けられないんですね。

To iu koto wa, ashita shiken o ukerarenai n' desu ne.

Which is to say, you won't be able to take the test tomorrow. Is that right?

Here are some other examples of this phrase:

A: あしたの朝は、空港まで友達を送りに行かなければいけないもので……。

Ashita no asa wa, kūkō made tomodachi o okuri ni ikanakereba ikenai mono de ...

Tomorrow morning I have to go to the airport to see a friend off, so ...

B: <u>ということ</u>は、あしたの授業には、出られないということですね。

To iu koto wa, ashita no jugyō ni wa, dararenai to iu koto desu ne.

That means, then, that you cannot attend tomorrow's class.

A: 私は、ああいうタイプの男性は嫌いなのよ。

Watashi wa, ā iu taipu no dansei wa kirai na no yo.

I really hate that type of man.

B: <u>ということは</u>、彼とは結婚しないのね。

To iu koto wa, kare to wa kekkon shinai no ne.

Which means, I suppose, that you aren't going to marry
him.

行こうか行くまいか／行こうが行くまいが

行こうか行くまいか (lit., whether to go or not) and 行こう
が行くまいが (lit., whether [understood subject] goes or not)
are exactly the same in structure except for the use of か
and が. The first indicates hesitation between two choices;
the second suggests that no matter which choice is made,
the result will be the same.

A: あしたのパーティ、行く？

Ashita no pātī, iku?

Are you going to the party tomorrow?

B: 今、<u>行こうか行くまいか</u>、迷ってるところ。

Ima, ikō ka iku mai ka, mayotte 'ru tokoro.

I am debating with myself whether I should go or not.

A: 彼女も行くの？

Kanojo mo iku no?

Is she going, too?

B: あんな人、<u>行こうが行くまいが</u>、私の知ったことじゃ
ないわよ。

*Anna hito, ikō ga iku mai ga, watashi no shitta koto ja
nai wa yo.*

Oh, her. Whether she goes or not has nothing to do
with me.

Both patterns can take verbs other than 行く, and both
can take subjects other than "I," although in the pattern
with か, using a subject other than "I" might be considered
to be an example of indirect discourse, where the speaker
is reporting the thoughts, feelings, or speech of another.

彼女は彼に会おうか会うまいか迷っている。

Kanojo wa kare ni aō ka au mai ka mayotte iru.

She can't make up her mind whether to meet him or
not.

Xに入って／Xになって

When X is a time period, に入（はい）って and になって are
interchangeable, as in 十月に入って and 十月になって.
Both suggest that some kind of change occurred after or
since the time period in question began.

十月に入って、やっと涼しい日が続くようになった。

Jūgatsu ni haitte, yatto suzushii hi ga tsuzuku yō ni natta.

Entering October, we finally began to have some cool
days.

日本人は、明治になって、ようやく許可なしで国内を移
動する自由を与えられた。

*Nihonjin wa, Meiji ni natte, yōyaku kyoka nashi de koku-
nai o idō suru jiyū o ataerareta.*

With the coming of the Meiji period, the Japanese people were finally given the freedom to move about
the country without special permission.

Xにあって

Xにあって simply means "right in the middle of X" or "dur-
ing the time period of X." No change from a previous time
period is suggested, as it is with に入って and になって.

この不況の時代にあって、あれだけの業績があげられる
ということは、驚くべきことだ。

*Kono fukyō no jidai ni atte, are dake no gyōseki ga age-
rareru to iu koto wa, odoroku beki koto da.*

To produce such results in the midst of this depression
is truly astounding.

職場にあっては、上司に口答えをすることなどとてもできなかったのだ。

Shokuba ni atte wa, jōshi ni kuchigotae o suru koto nado totemo dekinakatta no da.

To talk back to one's superior in a place of work was something I simply could not do.

〜と思った／〜かと思った／〜のかと思った

All of these phrases mean "I thought (mistakenly) that …," with only a slight difference in stress (the stronger on the right). They can be used interchangeably. The phrase is preceded by a dictionary form or a 〜た form.

音がしたから、誰か来たと思ったんだけど、風だった。

Oto ga shita kara, dare ka kita to omotta n' da kedo, kaze datta.

I heard a noise, so I thought someone had come, but it was the wind.

行かないの？　一緒に行くのかと思ってたわ。

Ikanai no? Issho ni iku no ka to omotte 'ta wa.

You're not going? I thought you'd be going with us.

あのお客さん、ハンドバッグをいろいろ見せてほしいって言うから一つぐらいは買うのかと思った。

Ano okyaku-san, handobaggu o iroiro misete hoshii tte iu kara hitotsu gurai wa kau no ka to omotta.

That customer asked to see various handbags, so I thought she was going to buy at least one.

〜と思ったら／〜かと思ったら

These two phrases, which essentially mean "Just as I thought (a certain thing had happened)," indicate that at the moment the speaker became aware of something, it had already ceased to exist or had changed into something else. The first part of the sentence, ending in 思ったら, refers to what the speaker perceived; the second part refers to what happened next or what resulted. In contrast to the phrase かと思った discussed immediately above, の cannot precede かと思ったら.

今来たかと思ったら、もう帰ってしまったの？　いったい、何しに来たのかしら。

Ima kita ka to omottara, mō kaette shimatta no? Ittai, nani shi ni kita no kashira.

I thought he had just come. You mean he's left already? I wonder why he came at all.

疲れているとみえて、今床についたと思ったら、もういびきをかいている。

Tsukarete iru to miete, ima toko ni tsuita to omottara, mō ibiki o kaite iru.

Looking tired, he had just gotten into bed I thought, when here he is already snoring.

〜が早いか

〜が早いか (roughly, "which is quicker?") can be used in place of 〜た（か）と思ったら, but the focus here is on what actually happened rather than on what the speaker perceived.

床につくが早いか、いびきをかいて眠っている。

Toko ni tsuku ga hayai ka, ibiki o kaite nemutte iru.

No sooner is he is bed than he is snoring.

彼は、朝食を食べるが早いか、家を飛び出していった。

Kare wa, chōshoku o taberu ga hayai ka, ie o tobidashite itta.

No sooner had he finished eating breakfast than he rushed out of the house.

～次第／～たら、すぐ

Both of these phrases indicate that one thing follows quickly upon another. ～次第 (which literally means "order" or "procedure") is preceded by a pre-ます form, as in 着き次第, and is characteristic of formal or written usage rather than casual conversation. It might be translated as "immediately upon" to bring out its formal nuance. In casual conversation, -たら、すぐ ("as soon as this, that") is more common.

A: ホテルの部屋の電話番号、分かりますか？

Hoteru no heya no denwa-bangō, wakarimasu ka.

Do you know the telephone number of your room at the hotel?

B: まだ分からないんですけれど、<u>分かり次第</u>そちらにご連絡しますので。

Mada wakaranai n' desu keredo, wakari-shidai sochira ni gorenraku shimasu no de.

I don't know it yet, but as soon as I do, I'll let you know.

A: 今、どこからかけてるの？

Ima, doko kara kakete 'ru no?

Where are you calling from?

B: 新幹線の中。東京駅に<u>着いたらすぐ</u>電話するから迎えに来て。

Shinkansen no naka. Tōkyō-eki ni tsuitara sugu denwa suru kara mukae ni kite.

From the Shinkan-sen (bullet train). I'll call you as soon as I get to Tokyo Station, so come and pick me up.

In the above examples, which involve requests, とすぐ cannot be used (see Shoji, pp. 99–114). とすぐ is possible only with habitual occurrences or routines.

いつも<u>帰るとすぐ</u>シャワーを浴びます。

Itsumo kaeru to sugu shawā o abimasu.

As soon as I get back, I always take a shower.

いつも、東京駅に<u>着くとすぐ</u>、電話だけはすることにしています。

Itsumo, Tōkyō-eki ni tsuku to sugu, denwa dake wa suru koto ni shite imasu.

I always call (my family) as soon as I arrive at Tokyo Station.

〜なり

〜なり has the same etymological roots as the verb 成る (なる ; "to become") and originally referred to a shape or condition. This original meaning gradually took on many forms, as we will see here. In the first two senses below, 〜なり is preceded by nouns or adjectives; the following three senses are preceded by verbs.

1. NounなりにV／NなりのN

Here なり has the meaning of a condition suitable or appropriate to the noun that precedes it and can be roughly translated as "to the best of N's ability" or "in keeping with N's character." It is often used to justify behavior or ward off criticism.

これでも、<u>私は私なりに</u>努力しているんです。

Kore de mo, watashi wa watashi nari ni doryoku shite iru n' desu.

It may not seem like it, but in my own way I am doing my best.

<u>彼には彼なりの</u>考え方があるのだから……。

Kare ni wa kare nari no kangaekata ga aru no da kara …

He has his own way of thinking, so …

2. Adjective ＋ なりに

This phrase is similar to the above in that it means "given

the character of the adjective" or "as one might expect from the character of the adjective." What follows after the phrase indicates what is expected. けれど can be substituted for なりに, though there would be an obvious change in focus.

このセーターは、高いなりにものがいい。

Kono sētā wa, takai nari ni mono ga ii.

The quality of this sweater is good, as you might expect from the price.

それなりのお礼はいたします。

Sore nari no orei wa itashimasu.

I'll compensate you accordingly (I'll express my thanks [gratitude] in an appropriate manner).

3. ～なり～なり ＋ sentence-ending verb

This pattern suggests alternatives to be acted upon. ～なり may be preceded by nouns or by verbs in dictionary form. The second verb can be the negative form of the verb that precedes the first なり or it can be a different verb.

とにかく、電話をするなりファックスを送るなり(して)すぐ知らせたほうがいい。

Tonikaku, denwa o suru nari fakkusu o okuru nari (shite) sugu shiraseta hō ga ii.

In any case, you should let them know right away, either by calling or by sending a fax.

会うなり会わないなり、はっきりしなさい。

Au nari awanai nari, hakkiri shinasai.

Whether you're going to meet her or not, make up your mind.

今夜なり明日の朝なり、ご都合のいい時にお電話ください。

Konya nari ashita no asa nari, gotsugō no ii toki ni odenwa kudasai.

Please call me tonight or tomorrow morning, whichever is convenient.

4. Verb なり + sentence-ending verb

This pattern indicates that two actions happen almost simultaneously.

淳子は、学校から帰ってくるなり泣き出した。

Junko wa, gakkō kara kaette kuru nari nakidashita.

Junko started to cry the moment she got home from school.

先生は、教室に入ってくるなり試験を始めた。

Sensei wa, kyōshitsu ni haitte kuru nari shiken o hajimeta.

The teacher had no sooner entered the classroom than she began the test.

5. 〜たなり

In this pattern, なり is preceded by a verb in the た form. The verb indicates that a change has taken place, and なり states that the condition brought about by the verb is still in effect, that no further change has occurred.

彼は、部屋に入ったなり一日中出てこなかった。

Kare wa, heya ni haitta nari ichinichi-jū dete konakatta.

He went into his room and didn't come out all day long.

あの子供の父親は、出稼ぎに行ったなり帰ってこないの
　だという。

Ano kodomo no chichioya wa, dekasegi ni itta nari kaette konai no da to iu.

They say that the child's father has gone to Tokyo as a seasonal worker and never come back.

Here, 〜なり may be replaced by the more colloquial 〜きり, again indicating that the condition brought about by the verb remains unchanged.

一郎は、アメリカに行ったきり、帰ってこない。

Ichirō wa, Amerika ni itta kiri, kaette konai.

Ichirō went to America and has never come back.

〜（た）まま／〜（た）きり／〜っぱなし

These three phrases are easily confused in that they all refer to an ongoing state or condition.

1. 〜（た）まま

まま indicates a condition that remains unchanged and might be translated "as is." The preceding た verb defines the condition. その etc. can come before まま if its meaning is understood from context.

> 読む暇がなくて、本を<u>買ったまま</u>置きっぱなしになっている。
>
> *Yomu hima ga nakute, hon o katta mama okippanashi ni natte iru.*
>
> Since I don't have any time to read, the books I bought are just left sitting there.

> 五千年も前の遭難者が、雪の中から<u>凍死したまま</u>の姿で発見された。
>
> *Gosennen mo mae no sōnan-sha ga, yuki no naka kara tōshi shita mama no sugata de hakken sareta.*
>
> A man who had met with a fatal accident some five thousand years ago was discovered unchanged (as he was) since freezing to death in the snow.

> 包まなくても、<u>そのまま</u>でけっこうです。
>
> *Tsutsumanakute mo, sono mama de kekkō desu.*
>
> You don't have to wrap it. It's fine as it is.

2. 〜たきり

〜たきり may be used in much the same way as 〜たまま, but the focus is placed on the discontinuation of the action indicated by the verb (きり meaning "cut-off"). In other words, something was done, but nothing occurred afterwards, and the original condition continues.

父は、徴兵された<u>きり</u>帰ってこなかったのです。

Chichi wa, chōhei sareta kiri, kaette konakatta no desu.

My father was drafted and never came back.

あの子ったら、お使いに行<u>ったきり</u>なのよ。

Ano ko ttara, otsukai ni itta kiri na no yo.

That little rascal! She went out on a errand and hasn't come back.

彼女と最後に会ったのは、昨年の暮れでした。<u>それっきり</u>音沙汰がないんです。

Kanojo to saigo ni atta no wa, sakunen no kure deshita. Sore kkiri otosata ga nai n' desu.

It was at the end of last year when I met her last. I haven't heard a word from her since.

3. 〜っぱなし

This phrase also refers to an ongoing condition, but it generally indicates an active ongoing state rather than a static one. It often connotes criticism, implying that the condition in question is the result of laziness, sloppiness, or carelessness.

<u>出しっぱなし</u>にしないで、読み終わったら本棚に戻しておきなさいよ。

Dashippanashi ni shinai de, yomiowattara hondana ni modoshite okinasai yo.

Don't leave them lying around like that. When you're done reading, put them back on the bookshelf.

手紙を<u>書きっぱなし</u>にして、出すのを忘れていた。

Tegami o kakippanashi ni shite, dasu no o wasurete ita.

I left the letter I wrote lying there and forgot to send it.

電気を<u>つけっぱなし</u>にしないでね。

Denki o tsukeppanashi ni shinai de ne.

Don't forget to turn the lights off. (Lit., Don't leave the light turned on.)

〜たとたんに

とたん can be paraphrased as "exactly at that moment," and thus the whole phrase (preceded by a た verb) is similar to なり and が早いか. However, in the case of A 〜たとたんに B, the subject of A and B cannot be the same, whereas the subject of A なり B is usually the same.

> ひかり31号は、彼が<u>飛び乗ったとたんに</u>／<u>飛び乗るが早いか</u>、発車した。
>
> *Hikari sanjūichi-gō wa, kare ga tobinotta totan ni/tobinoru ga hayai ka, hassha shita.*
>
> As soon as he jumped aboard, Hikari No. 31 (bullet train) departed.

> 彼は、部屋に荷物を<u>置くが早いか</u>／<u>置くなり</u>、また出ていってしまった。
>
> *Kare wa, heya ni nimotsu o oku ga hayai ka/oku nari, mata dete itte shimatta.*
>
> As soon as he had put his luggage in his room, he went out again.

おずおず（と）／おどおど（と）／びくびく（と）

Although these three onomatopoeic words are characterized by hesitation, nervousness, or timidity, there are certain differences.

1. おずおず（と）

This describes an action that is carried out with hesitation due to worry or lack of confidence. The action described is not expansive, but shrinking and withdrawn.

> 先生に名前を呼ばれた新入生は、<u>おずおずと</u>クラス全員の前に立ってあいさつをした。
>
> *Sensei ni namae o yobareta shinnyū-sei wa, ozuozu to kurasu zen'in no mae ni tatte aisatsu o shita.*

The new student whose name was called out by the teacher timidly stood in front of the class and introduced himself.

少年が<u>おずおずと</u>開いて見せた手のひらには、一羽のひな鳥がいた。

Shōnen ga ozuozu to hiraite miseta te no hira ni wa, ichiwa no hinadori ga ita.

Inside the hand that the boy timidly opened to show, there was a baby bird.

2. おどおど（と）

おどおど describes an action characterized by nervousness or restlessness due to tension or apprehension.

初めて屋外に連れ出された小犬は、<u>おどおどした</u>目つきで辺りを見回している。

Hajimete okugai ni tsuredasareta koinu wa, odoodo shita metsuki de atari o mimawashite iru.

The puppy, taken outside for the first time, is looking around him nervously.

カンニングをして呼び出された学生は、<u>おどおどと</u>教員室に入ってきた。

Kanningu o shite yobidasareta gakusei wa, odoodo to kyōin-shitsu ni haitte kita.

Having been summoned after cheating on a test, the student nervously entered the teachers' room.

3. びくびく（と）

The primary meaning of びくびく is to tremble physically, but here we are concerned with the psychological aspect of the word, which might be paraphrased as "an inner trembling." In this case, the fear comes from the expectation that something bad is going to happening. This fear may not be apparent to others, distinguishing this word from the otherwise very similar おどおど, which indicates an action always apparent on the surface. In the first example below, what the fugitive fears is that he will be apprehended.

> 自首してきた逃亡犯は、<u>びくびくしながら</u>暮らすことに
> 耐えられなくなったのだと言った。

> *Jishu shite kita tōbō-han wa, bikubiku shinagara kurasu koto ni taerarenaku natta no da to itta.*

> Shaking in his shoes, the fugitive turned himself over to the police, saying that he could no longer bear the life he was leading.

> 宿題をしてこなかったので、先生に名前を呼ばれたらど
> うしようかと、<u>びくびくしていた</u>。

> *Shukudai o shite konakatta no de, sensei ni namae o yobaretara dō shiyō ka to, bikubiku shite ita.*

> Because I didn't do my homework, I was worried to death that the teacher might call my name.

途中／中途

Although these two compounds are often translated as "halfway," they are not necessarily interchangeable. 途中 simply means "on one's way to" or "in the middle of," while 中途 implies that something is "half done," that it has been left uncompleted or unfinished. It has a negative tone.

> 仕事の<u>途中</u>で人に来られてしまったもので、予定通り仕
> 上げることができなかった。

> *Shigoto no tochū de hito ni korarete shimatta mono de, yotei-dōri shiageru koto ga dekinakatta.*

> Because someone came to see me in the middle of my work, I was unable to finish it as planned.

> 渋谷駅に行く<u>途中</u>（<u>で</u>）竹下さんに会いましたけど、元気
> そうでした。

> *Shibuya-eki ni iku tochū (de) Takeshita-san ni aimashita kedo, genkisō deshita.*

On my way to Shibuya Station, I saw Ms. Takeshita.
    She looked fine.

資金が足りず、工事が<u>中途</u>のままになっている。

Shikin ga tarizu, kōji ga chūto no mama ni natte iru.

Due to a lack of funds, the construction remains unfin-
    ished.

彼女は、仕事が<u>中途でも</u>、時間が来るとさっさと帰って
    しまうんですよ。

*Kanojo wa, shigoto ga chūto de mo, jikan ga kuru to sassa
    to kaette shimau n' desu yo.*

When office hours are over, she just ups and goes
    home, even if her work is only half done.

中途半端 is also commonly used in various situations, with
its negative implications even clearer than 中途.

彼女は、二つの文化の中で育ったので、どちらも半分半
    分で<u>中途半端</u>になっているところがあるようだ。

*Kanojo wa, futatsu no bunka no naka de sodatta no de,
    dochira mo hanbun hanbun de chūto-hanpa ni natte
    iru tokoro ga aru yō da.*

Because she was raised in two cultures, with each half
    learned, in some ways it seems she knows neither
    completely.

あの修理店は<u>中途半端</u>な仕事しかしないから行かないほ
    うがいいと、友達に言われた。

*Ano shūri-ten wa chūto-hanpa na shigoto shika shinai
    kara ikanai hō ga ii to, tomodachi ni iwareta.*

My friend told me, "You'd better not go to that repair
    shop, because they do nothing but lousy jobs."

山田君は、いつも四時半になると、帰っていってしまうんで
    す。仕事が<u>中途半端</u>でも、気にならないらしいですね。

*Yamada-kun wa, itsumo yoji-han ni naru to, kaette itte
    shimau n' desu. Shigoto ga chūto-hanpa de mo, ki ni
    naranai rashii desu ne.*

Yamada always goes on home at 4:30. It seems that he doesn't mind if the work is only half done.

彼の考え方が<u>中途半端</u>なので、いらいらします。
Kare no kangaekata ga chūto-hanpa na no de, iraira shimasu.
His thinking is so half-baked that I get frustrated.

（今にして）思えば

今にして思えば ("now that I think about it") is followed by a description of something that happened or existed in the past and shows the speaker's emotional involvement and subjective interpretation of the matter. Although the speaker did not take the matter seriously at the time, he or she now becomes aware of its value or significance. This statement may imply regret, compassion, or some other such emotion.

<u>今にして思えば</u>、あんな人の口車に乗った自分が恥ずかしい。

Ima ni shite omoeba, anna hito no kuchiguruma ni notta jibun ga hazukashii.

Now that I think about, I'm ashamed of being taken in by the smooth talk of someone like that.

アルバイトと勉強ばかりでデートをする暇もないような大学時代だったけど、<u>今にして思えば</u>、なつかしい。

Arubaito to benkyō bakari de dēto o suru hima mo nai yō na daigaku-jidai datta kedo, ima ni shite omoeba, natsukashii.

My college days where nothing but study and part-time work, with no time for dating, but thinking back now, I have some good memories.

～っぽい／らしい

～っぽい is attached to a noun and indicates that 1) something is tinged with a particular color, or 2) someone or something has a unique trait, manner, or characteristic.

A: (刑事) その女性は、どんな服装をしていましたか。

(Keiji) Sono josei wa, donna fukusō o shite imashita ka.

(Detective) What was the woman wearing?

B: (目撃者) 黄色っぽい色のブラウスの上に、白いセーターを着ていたと思います。

(Mokugeki-sha) Kiiroppoi iro no burausu no ue ni, shiroi sētā o kite ita to omoimasu.

(Witness) She was wearing a yellowish blouse with a white sweater over it, I think.

あの学生は、飽きっぽいので何をやってもだめなんです。

Ano gakusei wa, akippoi no de nani o yatte mo dame nan desu.

Because that student easily loses interest, he cannot achieve anything.

うちの上司は、怒りっぽいのが玉に瑕です。

Uchi no jōshi wa, okorippoi no ga tama ni kizu desu.

The only drawback of my boss is that he easily loses his temper.

近頃、彼女はひがみっぽくなった。

Chikagoro, kanojo wa higamippoku natta.

These days she seems to think the whole world is against her.

彼女が、見かけはいかにも女らしいのに、男っぽい話し方をするのでびっくりした。

Kanojo ga, mikake wa ikanimo onna rashii no ni, otokoppoi hanashikata o suru no de bikkuri shita.

She looks so feminine on the surface, I was surprised that she talks like a man.

この頃、秋子は大人っぽいことを言うようになった。

Kono goro, Akiko wa otonappoi koto o iu yō ni natta.

Recently, Akiko has started to talk like an adult.

In cases where a quality or manner is seen as typical, ideal, or as expected by society at large, らしい is used. In the opposite case, くせに is used.

私は、<u>男らしい</u>人が好き。
Watashi wa, otoko rashii hito ga suki.
I like the manly type.

<u>日本人らしい</u>考え方ね。
Nihon-jin rashii kangaekata ne.
It's a typically Japanese way of thinking.

もっと<u>女の子らしく</u>しろと母に言われた。
Motto onna no ko rashiku shiro to haha ni iwareta.
I was told by my mother to behave more like a girl is supposed to behave.

あの子、男の子の<u>くせに</u>すぐ泣くのよ。
Ano ko, otoko no ko no kuse ni sugu naku no yo.
He cries easily, not like a boy at all.

Other examples of ～っぽい:

湿っぽい空気／話
shimeppoi kūki/hanashi
damp air / a depressing story

ぐちっぽい人
guchippoi hito
a complainer

ほこりっぽい部屋
hokorippoi heya
a dusty room

水っぽいお酒
mizuppoi osake
watery sake

安っぽい洋服
yasuppoi yōfuku
cheap-looking clothes

気障っぽい話し方
kizappoi hanashikata
a pretentious or affected way of talking

〜じみた

〜じみた is derived from the verb 染みる（じみる）, which has the primary meaning of "to dye" and secondary meanings of "to stain," "to smack of," "to look like," and "to act like." It is the seconary meanings that are carried over into the suffix 〜じみた, which usually has a negative connotation.

そんな<u>年寄りじみた</u>言い方、しないで。
Sonna toshiyori-jimita iikata, shinai de.
Don't talk like an old man in that way.

いい年してそんな<u>子供じみた</u>ことをするの、やめなさいよ。
Ii toshi shite sonna kodomo-jimita koto o suru no, yame-nasai yo.
Think of your age and stop acting like a child.

部屋の中には、<u>あかじみた</u>シャツだけが置きっぱなしになっていた。
Heya no naka ni wa, aka-jimita shatsu dake ga okippa-nashi ni natte ita.
Only a filthy shirt was left lying in the room.

Xだらけ／Xまみれ

だらけ indicates 1) that there is a lot of X, or 2) that X is scattered completely over a surface. The connotations are negative. まみれ indicates that X is smeared over a surface, making it filthy. This meaning overlaps with the second meaning of だらけ, though they each, of course, retain their own nuances. Another difference between the two is that the X in Xだらけ may refer to either countable or uncountable items, while the X in Xまみれ refers generally only to uncountable items. In the first two examples below, the two are basically interchangeable.

子供達が<u>泥まみれになって</u>遊んでいる。

Kodomo-tachi ga doro-mamire ni natte asonde iru.

The children are playing, all covered with mud.

壁には、<u>血まみれになった</u>テロの犠牲者たちの写真が、何枚もはられていた。

Kabe ni wa, chi-mamire ni natta tero no giseisha-tachi no shashin ga, nan-mai mo hararete ita.

Many photographs of the bloody victims of terrorism were posted on the wall.

あの俳優、<u>借金だらけ</u>なんですって。信じられる？

Ano haiyū, shakkin-darake nan desu tte. Shinjirareru?

I heard that the actor is loaded with debts. Can you believe it?

<u>砂だらけ</u>の足で家に入らないで。

Suna-darake no ashi de ie ni hairanai de.

Don't come into the house with your feet covered with sand.

こんなに<u>間違いだらけ</u>の作文、どうやって<u>直す</u>の？

Konna ni machigai-darake no sakubun, dō yatte naosu no?

How can I correct a composition so full of mistakes like this?

村人たちが<u>傷だらけ</u>になって倒れていた旅人を助けた。

Murabito-tachi ga kizu-darake ni natte taorete ita tabibito o tasuketa.

The villagers came to the rescue of a traveler who had collapsed with his body covered with wounds.

煩（わずら）わしい

煩わしい, which might be translated as "troublesome," "irksome," or "vexing," describes the speaker's feelings in regard to a certain matter, usually one that is complicated and difficult to deal with, such as human relations in the workplace.

髪の毛が長いと、煩わしいからいやなんです。

Kami no ke ga nagai to, wazurawashii kara iya nan desu.

I don't like long hair because it's so troublesome.

あの人がいると、何故か分からないけど、煩わしいんです。

Ano hito ga iru to, naze ka wakaranai kedo, wazurawashii n' desu.

I don't know why, but I feel so exasperated when he is around.

会社の煩わしい人間関係がいやになったから、辞めたんです。

Kaisha no wazurawashii ningen-kankei ga iya ni natta kara, yameta n' desu.

Because I hated the troublesome human relations in the office, I quit.

忙しくて、そんな煩わしいことにはかかわってる暇なんてないですよ。

Isogashikute, sonna wazurawashii koto ni wa kakawatte 'ru hima nante nai desu yo.

I am too busy to get involved in a troublesome matter like that.

うるさい

うるさい may be translated as "noisy," but the cause of annoyance is not always sound. When it is sound, うるさい indicates that the sound is irritating. Secondarily, the word indicates that somebody or something is bothering the speaker by being persistent, unrelenting, or fussy.

夕べは、隣の部屋の話し声が<u>うるさくて</u>眠れなかった。

Yūbe wa, tonari no heya no hanashi-goe ga urusakute, nemurenakatta.

I wasn't able to sleep last night because the people next door were talking so loud.

彼が、下の換気装置の音が<u>うるさくて</u>、いらいらすると言っています。

Kare ga, shita no kanki-sōchi no oto ga urusakute, iraira suru to itte imasu.

He says that the noise from the downstairs' ventilator irritates him.

<u>うるさい</u>なあ。だめって言ったらだめなの。

Urusai nā. Dame tte ittara dame na no.

Stop nagging. If I say "no," I mean "no."

余り<u>うるさく</u>すると、連れていかないよ。

Amari urusaku suru to, tsurete ikanai yo.

If you keep bothering me, I won't take you along.

あの上司は、<u>うるさい</u>ことばかり言うので嫌われている。

Ano jōshi wa, urusai koto bakari iu no de kirawarete iru.

That boss isn't liked because he's always fussing over something.

When the cause of annoyance is a noise or voice, やかましい may be more commonly used.

隣のパーティーが<u>やかましくて</u>、眠れない。

Tonari no pāti ga yakamashikute, nemurenai.

I can't sleep because of the ruckus from the party next door.

工事の音が<u>やかましい</u>んですけど、窓を閉めてもらえま
せんか。

*Kōji no oto ga yakamashii n' desu kedo, mado o shimete
moraemasen ka.*

The noise from the construction work is getting on my
nerves. Would you mind closing the window?

せっかく

せっかく is used, first, to express appreciation for someone's
kindness or goodwill. Second, it may indicate disappointment that one's goodwill was not appreciated by the party
on the receiving end. Third, it may simply indicate disappointment that one's efforts in some endeavor did not result in success.

<u>せっかく</u>のご厚意、ありがたくお受けします。

Sekkaku no gokōi, arigataku ouke shimasu.

I am very grateful for your solicitude on my behalf.

<u>せっかく</u>招待してくれたんだから、行ったほうがいいよ。

Sekkaku shōtai shite kureta n' da kara, itta hō ga ii yo.

Since they so kindly invited you, I think you should go.

<u>せっかく</u>晴れたんだから、散歩にでも行こうよ。

Sekkaku hareta n' da kara, sanpo ni de mo ikō yo.

Since the weather has cleared up, let's take advantage
of it and go for a walk.

<u>せっかく</u>来てくださったのに、留守をしていてごめんな
さい。

Sekkaku kite kudasatta no ni, rusu o shite ite gomennasai.

I'm sorry that I wasn't in when you so kindly called.

欲しがっていたから<u>せっかく</u>買ってきてあげたのに、着てみようともしないんだから。

Hoshigatte ita kara sekkaku katte kite ageta no ni, kite miyō to mo shinai n' da kara.

Since you wanted it, I went out of my way to get you one, and now you won't even try it on.

<u>せっかく</u>のお休みだったのに、仕事をさせられてしまった。

Sekkaku no oyasumi datta no ni, shigoto o saserarete shimatta.

Although it was supposed to be my day off, I was called in to do some work anyway.

<u>せっかく</u>の旅行が台風で台なしになって、本当にがっかりした。

Sekkaku no ryokō ga taifū de dai-nashi ni natte, hontō ni gakkari shita.

The typhoon completely wrecked the trip I had planned. What a disappointment!

わざわざ

わざわざ may be used in situations similar to that of せっかく, but they are not always interchangable. Even if they are used in the same situation, the speaker's focus will be different. わざわざ refers to a physical act or the time spent for that act, while せっかく mainly refers to the doer's kindness or goodwill.

<u>わざわざ</u>切符を買いに行ったのに、売り切れてしまっていたのでがっかりした。

Wazawaza kippu o kai ni itta no ni, urikirete shimatte ita no de gakkari shita.

Though I went all the way there to buy a ticket, I was disappointed to find them all sold out.

わざわざ高い入場料を払って入ったのに、ヤンキースが
　負けちゃった。

*Wazawaza takai nyūjō-ryō o haratte haitta no ni, Yankīsu
ga makechatta.*

Here I paid a mint to buy these expensive tickets, but
the Yankees lost.

Although せっかく could be substituted for わざわざ in
the sentences above (with the aforementioned change in
focus), it could not in the following dialogue because appre-
ciaton is being shown specifically for the time and trouble
it took to bring over the mail, not for a general act of goodwill.

A: お宅の郵便が間違って配送されたもので。

Otaku no yūbin ga machigatte haisō sareta mono de.

Your mail got delivered to us by mistake, so ...

B: あ、どうもわざわざすみません。

A, dōmo wazawaza sumimasen.

Thank you for taking the trouble.

よほど／よっぽど

よほど and よっぽど basically mean "by far" and are used
for comparison. They are interchangeable, but the latter is
more emphatic and typical of the spoken language.

A: あれ、どう？

Are, dō?

How about that one?

B: あれ？　だめ。これのほうがよっぽどいいよ。

Are? Dame. Kore no hō ga yoppodo ii yo.

That one? No way. This is much better.

Either word may indicate difficulty in making a decision
or choice.

A: あの赤い車、買ったの？

Ano akai kuruma, katta no?

Did you buy that red car?

B: ん。気に入ったから、<u>よほど</u>買おうかと思ったんだけどね、赤いのは、やっぱりちょっとはで過ぎるよ。

N. Ki ni itta kara, yohodo kaō ka to omotta n' da kedo ne, akai no ha, yappari chotto hade sugiru yo.

Yeah, I liked it a lot, so I was really thinking of buying it, but red is a little too flashy after all.

よほど and よっぽど can indicate speculation based on observation or secondhand information.

A: 彼、もう居眠りしてるよ。

Kare, mō inemuri shite 'ru yo.

He's already dozing off.

B: <u>よっぽど</u>疲れているんだね。

Yoppodo tsukarete iru n' da ne.

He must be really tired.

In this example, B is offering an opinion based on A's observation, but in the following example, the observation is made by the speaker.

もう居眠りを始めたところを見ると、<u>よほど</u>疲れているらしい。

Mō inemuri o hajimeta tokoro o miru to, yohodo tsukarete iru rashii.

He must be really tired. He's already started to doze off.

かえって

かえって is often translated as "rather" or "all the more," but "instead" or "contrary to expectation" would be more accurate in AかえってB patterns in which B indicates a result or outcome that is opposed to, or different from, the speaker's or common expectation.

A: 薬飲んだ？

Kusuri nonda?

You take the medicine?

B: 薬を飲んだら、<u>かえって</u>気分が悪くなっちゃた。

Kusuri o nondara, kaette kibun ga waruku natchatta.

I took it, but I feel worse instead.

かえって is often used in combination with こちらこそ ("I am the one who …") in polite expressions such as the following:

A: 手伝っていただいて、ありがとうございます。

Tetsudatte itadaite, arigatō gozaimasu.

Thank you very much for helping out.

B: いいえ。<u>かえって</u>こちらこそごちそうになってしまって。

Iie. Kaette kochira koso gochisō ni natte shimatte.

Oh, don't mention it. Rather I should thank you for the lovely meal.

AことはB（けど／が）C

In this pattern, A and B are the same word: for example, いくことはいくけど. A rough English equivalent might be, "As to the matter of going, well, I am going, but" or, more simply, "I *am* going, but." This partially acknowledges the validity of what the other party has said, but then goes on to point out that there are others factors to consider.

A: どうしたの？　買い物にいったんじゃなかったの？

Dō shita no? Kaimono ni itta n' ja nakatta no?

What happened? I thought you went shopping.

B: <u>行ったことは行ったんだけど</u>、あんまり込んでいるから帰ってきちゃったの。

Itta koto wa itta n' da kedo, anmari konde iru kara kaette kitchatta no.

I did go, but it was so crowded that I came back.

A: 新しいレストラン、どうだった？　おいしかった？

Atarashii resutoran, dō datta? Oishikatta?

How was the new restaurant? Was it good?

B: <u>おいしいことはおいしいけど</u>、私にはちょっと高すぎる。

Oishii koto wa oishii kedo, watashi ni wa chotto takasugiru.

It was good all right, but a little too expensive for me.

という

という is used in various ways.

1. As an abbreviated form of ということです, to indicate a hearsay statement.

オランウータンは、この森に棲息しているという。

Oranūtan wa, kono mori ni seisoku shite iru to iu.

They say that orangutans inhabit this forest.

2. To introduce something new or unfamiliar.

この辺に、カルネ<u>という</u>喫茶店がありますか。

Kono hen ni, Karune to iu kissaten ga arimasu ka.

Is there a coffee shop called Karune around here?

山中さん<u>という</u>男の方が、お見えになっていらっしゃいますが。

Yamanaka-san to iu otoko no kata ga, omie ni natte irasshaimasu ga.

A man by the name of Yamanaka is here to see you.

3. To connect a modifier to a noun or noun phrase, especially when the modifier is hearsay or a question.

お隣から、<u>今朝届いたという</u>、新鮮な<u>野菜</u>をいただいた。

Otonari kara, kesa todoita to iu, shinsen na yasai o itadaita.

The neighbors gave us some fresh vegetables they say arrived this morning.

日本人のルーツがどこにあるのか<u>ということ</u>に関しては、様々な説が出されている。

Nihon-jin no rūtsu ga doko ni aru no ka to iu koto ni kan-shite wa, samazama na setsu ga dasarete iru.

Concerning the matter of where the Japanese originated, various theories have been suggested.

The phrase という is not always translated, though it is commonly used when the preceding modifier is lengthy.

4. To set off a general concept or a word for definition.

死<u>という</u>ものは、どうとらえるべきなのか。私はこの問いに答えられなかった。

Shi to iu mono wa, dō toraeru beki na no ka. Watashi wa kono toi ni kotaerarenakatta.

How are we to grasp the concept of death? I was unable to answer this question.

愛<u>という</u>ものは、不思議なものです。

Ai to iu mono wa, fu-shigi na mono desu.

Love is a mysterious thing.

5. When という is followed by ような, the following question becomes uncertain or vague.

彼も、あした来る<u>というような</u>ことを言っていました。

Kare mo, ashita kuru to iu yō na koto o itte imashita.

He said something about coming tomorrow, too.

悪い流感がはやっている<u>というような</u>ことを聞いたのですけれど、そちらは大丈夫ですか。

Warui ryūkan ga hayatte iru to iu yō na koto o kiita no desu keredo, sochira wa daijōbu desu ka.

I heard something about a bad flu going around. Are you doing all right?

6. Idiomatic uses.

実は、あしたまでにしあげないといけない仕事があるんですよ。それに、夜は、結婚披露宴に行かなきゃならないし。<u>というわけで／という次第で</u>、今日は、お先に失礼します。

Jitsu wa, ashita made ni shiagenai to ikenai shigoto ga aru n' desu yo. Sore ni, yoru wa, kekkon-hirōen ni ikanakya naranai shi. To iu wake de/to iu shidai de, kyō wa, osaki ni shitsurei shimasu.

To tell the truth, I have some work that I have to finish by tomorrow. In addition to that, I have to go to a wedding reception tonight. So, with that being the situation, you'll understand if I leave early today.

では、<u>ということで</u>。また連絡します。

Dewa, to iu koto de. Mata renraku shimasu.

Well, then, we'll leave it at that. I'll contact you again later.

彼女は、おとなしい<u>というよりは</u>、むしろ暗い感じです。

Kanojo wa, otonashii to iu yori wa, mushiro kurai kanji desu.

Rather than being quiet, she impresses me as being gloomy.

というより is often used with むしろ or どちらかといえば for comparison or selection.

A: そちらは？　ビール？

Sochira wa? Bīru?

How about you? Beer?

B: <u>というよりは</u>……<u>どちらかといえば</u>お酒のほうがいいんだけど。

To iu yori wa … dochira ka to ieba osake no hō ga ii n' da kedo.

No, rather than beer … I actually prefer sake if I have a choice.

今ごろ／今ごろになって

今ごろ shares with このごろ the meaning "these days," but it has another meaning that it does not share, which is "about now" or "right now." It is often related to the speaker's thoughts about what is happening at this moment somewhere else. 今ごろになって carries this a step further, usually in a critical fashion, as we will see below.

『<u>今ごろ</u>の若い者は何を考えているのかさっぱり分からない』と、祖父がぼやいています。

"Ima goro no wakai mono wa nani o kangaete iru no ka sappari wakaranai" to, sofu ga boyaite imasu.

My grandfather often complains, saying, "I don't understand what young people these days are thinking."

A: あの人、<u>今ごろ</u>、何してるかな。

Ano hito, ima goro, nani shite 'ru ka na.

I wonder what he is doing (right) now.

B: 今、向こうは朝の十時ごろだから、もう仕事してるんじゃない？

Ima, mukō wa asa no jūji goro da kara, mō shigoto shite 'ru n' ja nai?

Now it's about 10:00 in the morning over there, so he's already working, I guess.

A: あと十分早く来ていたら、<u>今ごろ</u>は、もう東京駅に着いていたのに……。

Ato juppun hayaku kite itara, ima goro wa, mō Tōkyō-eki ni tsuite ita no ni ...

If you had come ten minutes earlier, we'd be at Tokyo Station by now.

B: ごめんなさい。寝坊しちゃったのよ。

Gomennasai. Nebō shichatta no yo.

Sorry! I overslept.

A: 去年の<u>今ごろ</u>は、箱根に行ってたんだよね。

Kyonen no ima goro wa, Hakone ni itte 'ta n' da yo ne.

About this time last year, we were in Hakone, weren't we.

B: 覚えてる。桜がきれいだったわね。

Oboete 'ru. Sakura ga kirei datta wa ne.

I remember. The cherry blossoms were lovely, weren't they.

今ごろになって is usually followed by an ending that expresses the speaker's frustration, regret, or a complaint, implying "It's too late now … "

A: 若いうちに、もっとまじめに英語の勉強しておけばよかった……。

Wakai uchi ni, motto majime ni Eigo no benkyō shite okeba yokatta …

I should have studied English more seriously when I was young.

B: <u>今ごろになって</u>そんなこといっても、もう手遅れよ。

Ima goro ni natte sonna koto itte mo, mō teokure yo.

It's a little late to be saying that now.

A: 切符、売り切れだって。あの試合、見たかったのにがっかりだなあ。

Kippu, urikire datte. Ano shiai, mitakatta no ni gakkari da nā.

All tickets sold out, I hear. What a letdown! I wanted to see that game.

B: <u>今ごろになって</u>そんなこと言ったって、どうにもならないよ。

Ima goro ni natte sonna koto itta tte, dō ni mo naranai yo.

It's a little late to be complaining now. There's nothing you can do about it.

以（もっ）て

以（もっ）て is characteristic of the written language or of formal or official usage. In less formal situations, で may replace it.

1. To end or close an event.

本日は、<u>これをもって</u>閉会といたします。

Honjitsu wa, kore o motte heikai to itashimasu.

Today we hereby bring these proceedings (this conference etc.) to a close.

2. To tell "with what" or "by means of what."

書面を<u>もって</u>、失礼します。

Shomen o motte, shitsurei shimasu.

I apologize for communicating by letter. (I know I should personally come to see you, but I cannot.)

皆の力を<u>もって</u>すれば、不可能なことではない。

Mina no chikara o motte sureba, fu-kanō na koto de wa nai.

We can do it if everybody cooperates (lit., puts their strength into it).

3. To spell out the subject.

彼の研究を<u>もって</u>学界の定説としている。

Kare no kenkyū o motte gakkai no teisetsu to shite iru.

His research has become the establish theory in the academic world.

Verb + しかない

When しかない follows a noun, as in 本（ほん）しかない, it indicates that there is nothing but a 本. When it follows a verb, it indicates that there is only one choice, that represented by the verb.

A: 私は、明日もあさっても忙しくてだめ。

Watashi wa, ashita mo asatte mo isogashikute dame.

Both tomorrow and the day after are no good for me. I'm too busy.

B: そう。それじゃあ、きょう<u>行くしかない</u>ね。

Sō. Sore jā, kyō iku shika nai ne.

All right. In that case, we have no other choice but to go today.

アラスカに行こうと思ったけど、休暇が取れそうにないから、今年は<u>あきらめるしかない</u>ようだ。

Arasuka ni ikō to omotta kedo, kyūka ga toresō ni nai kara, kotoshi wa akirameru shika nai yō da.

I was thinking of going to Alaska, but it seems I won't be able to get off, so I'll guess I have to give it up this year.

どうも

どうも is commonly used within expressions of appreciation or apology, such as as どうもありがとうございます and どうもすみません, but it is also used with a negative verb ending to indicate that the speaker is having difficulty in solving a problem or in understanding or doing something, although an effort is being made to do so.

<u>どうも</u>、あの人の言うことが信用できないのです。

Dōmo, ano hito no iu koto ga shinyō dekinai no desu.

Really, I just can't believe what that guy says.

この問題、<u>どうも</u>分からないんですけど、どうやって解けばいいんですか。

Kono mondai, dōmo wakaranai n' desu kedo, dō yatte tokeba ii n' desu ka.

Really, I can't understand this problem. How should I go about solving it?

どうしても〜ない indicates that something is impossible even if the speaker has tried hard. The speaker may, in fact have already given up.

> この問題、<u>どうしても</u>解け<u>ない</u>んです。どうやればいいか教えてください。
>
> *Kono mondai, dō shite mo tokenai n' desu. Dō yareba ii ka oshiete kudasai.*
>
> I can't solve this problem, no matter how hard I try. Please tell me how to do it.

どうにも／どうとも

どうにも and どうとも look similar, but the former takes a negative verb ending to indicate that there is no possibility at all, while the latter is used with a potential ending to indicate that there is more than one possibility.

> もう、<u>どうにも</u>なら<u>ない</u>。
>
> *Mō, dō ni mo naranai.*
>
> We can't do anything about it now.

> いくらやっても、<u>どうにも</u>出来<u>ない</u>なら、やめたほうがいい。
>
> *Ikura yatte mo, dō ni mo dekinai nara, yameta hō ga ii.*
>
> If you just can't do it no matter how hard you try, you'd better give up.

> この文書は、<u>どうとも解釈できる</u>と思う。
>
> *Kono bunsho wa, dō to mo kaishaku dekiru to omou.*
>
> I think you can interpret this sentence in any way you like.

> <u>どうとも、</u>自分の好きにしなさい。
>
> *Dō to mo, jibun no suki ni shinasai.*
>
> Do whatever you like.

〜まい

〜まい is used with a dictionary form of a verb, and it always expresses a negative idea.

1. When the subject is the first person, it indicates a strong intention not to do something.

   あんな嫌なやつとは、もう二度と口を<u>きくまい</u>。

   Anna iya na yatsu to wa, mō nido to kuchi o kiku mai.

   I will never talk to that creep ever again.

   わたしは、もう二度と彼に<u>会うまい</u>と心に決めた。

   Watashi wa, mō nido to kare ni au mai to kokoro ni kimeta.

   I made up my mind never to see him again.

2. When the subject is other than the first person, 〜まい expresses a negative opinion about a future matter.

   残念ながら、この雨林が再び緑に包まれることは<u>あるまい</u>。

   Zannen nagara, kono urin ga futatabi midori ni tsutsumareru koto wa aru mai.

   To our regret, this rain forest will never be covered with green again.

   彼ならそんな事は<u>言うまい</u>と思ったのに。

   Kare nara sonna koto wa iu mai to omotta no ni.

   I never thought he would say anything like that.

3. N じゃあるまいし: By N じゃあるまいし, the speaker is implying that while the subject is not N, he or she is acting like N, which is not proper. The expression is commonly used in scolding.

   <u>子供じゃあるまいし</u>、自分の部屋ぐらい自分で片付けなさい。

   Kodomo ja aru mai shi, jibun no heya gurai jibun de katazukenasai.

You are not a child any more, you know. You should clean (straighten) up your room by yourself.

<u>日曜日じゃあるまいし</u>、さっさと起きないと学校に遅れ
ますよ。

Nichiyō-bi ja aru mai shi, sassa to okinai to gakkō ni okuremasu yo.

Today's not Sunday, you know. Get up this instant or you'll be late for school.

くらい／ぐらい

くらい／ぐらい is used to show degrees and amounts. Following are some of these usages.

1. To show approximate amount or number.

百ドル<u>ぐらい</u>の贈り物
hyaku-doru gurai no okurimono
a present of about $100

一時間<u>ぐらい</u>
ichiji-kan gurai
about an hour

それ<u>くらい</u>
sore kurai
about that much

2. To show an extent or degree.

我慢できない<u>くらい</u>痛かった。
Gaman dekinai kurai itakatta.
The pain was unbearable. (It hurt to the extent that it was unbearable.)

休む暇もない<u>くらい</u>忙しい。

Yasumu hima mo nai kurai isogashii.

I'm so busy I don't have time to take a rest.

3. くらいなら: To show the speaker's disgust about what was suggested or offered for consideration.

あの課長に<u>謝る</u><u>くらいなら</u>、僕は会社を辞めるよ。

Ano kachō ni ayamaru kurai nara, boku wa kaisha o yameru yo.

If it comes to apologizing to the section chief, I'll quit the company.

4. To show the speaker's least expectations.

一年に一度、温泉に行く<u>くらい</u>の時間の余裕が欲しいですね。

Ichinen ni ichido, onsen ni iku kurai no jikan no yoyū ga hoshii desu ne.

I'd like to have at least enough spare time to go to a hot spring once a year.

手紙を書く時間はなくても、電話をかけること<u>ぐらい</u>はできるでしょうに。

Tegami o kaku jikan wa nakute mo, denwa o kakeru koto gurai wa dekiru deshō ni.

Even though she doesn't have time to write, she should at least have time to call.

〜がる

〜がる is basically used in two ways. Its noun form is 〜がり.

1. To indicate a pretense or pose.

A: 一人で持てるなんて<u>強がって</u>たけど、大丈夫かな。

Hitori de moteru nante tsuyogatte 'ta kedo, daijōbu ka na.

He acted like it was nothing, saying he could carry it by himself, but I wonder.

B: 大丈夫だと思うけど、あの人、<u>強がり</u>を言いすぎるのよね。

Daijōbu da to omou kedo, ano hito, tsuyogari o iisugiru no yo ne.

I think he can manage it, but he does put up a bold front too easily, you know.

2. To show the subject's feelings or desire based on observation or an impression. To describe what is happening now, the verb ending should be the stative/resultative ～ている form, as in the last example.

<u>いやがってる</u>のに、むりやり芸をしこむなんて動物がかわいそうだ。

Iyagatte 'ru no ni, muriyari gei o shikomu nante dōbutsu ga kawaisō da.

It's cruel to force animals to do tricks when they don't want to.

君がニューヨークに帰ってしまったので、ジムが<u>寂しがってる</u>よ。

Kimi ga Nyūyōku ni kaette shimatta no de, Jimu ga sabishigatte 'ru yo.

Jim misses you since you went back to New York.

3. To show a tendency or natural inclination.

猫は本能的に水を<u>怖がる</u>ものなんですって。

Neko wa honnō-teki ni mizu o kowagaru mono nan desu tte.

I hear that cats are instinctively afraid of water.

彼のいいところは、子供を<u>可愛がる</u>ことです。

Kare no ii tokoro wa, kodomo o kawaigaru koto desu.

His good point is that he is fond of children.

圭子は、いつも忙しがっている。

Keiko wa itsumo isogashigatte iru.

Keiko is always running around (saying she is busy.)

まみさんは、寒がりやなんですか。

Mami-san wa, samugari-ya nan desu ka.

Mami, are you sensitive to cold weather?

Compare the following sentences:

父は[すぐ文句を言うので、]みんなにうるさがられている。

Chichi wa (sugu monku o iu no de,) minna ni urusagararete iru.

[父がすぐ文句を言うので、]みんながうるさがっている。

(Chichi ga sugu monku o iu no de,) minna ga urusagatte iru.

Because my father is quick to find fault, everybody finds it annoying.

ことにしている／ことになっている

ことにした refers to the speaker's decision, while ことになった refers to someone else's decision.

今年は、北海道にスキーに行くことにしました。

Kotoshi wa, Hokkaidō ni suki ni iku koto ni shimashita.

This year I've decided to go to Hokkaido to ski.

来月、大阪に赴任することになりました。

Raigetsu, Ōsaka ni funin suru koto ni narimashita.

I have been assigned to work in Osaka from next month.

When the ending is ～ている、ことにしている refers to the speaker's routine or habitual behavior, and ことになっている refers to a social custom or regulation.

毎日、五時に起きることにしています。

Mainichi, goji ni okiru koto ni shite imasu.

I make it a habit to get up at five o'clock every morning.

日本の家には、靴をぬいで<u>入ることになっています</u>。

Nihon no ie ni wa, kutsu o nuide hairu koto ni natte imasu.

In Japan, it is the custom to take off one's shoes before entering a house.

Aは、Bほどのことはない

Aは、Bほどのことはない indicates that 1) A is less in quantity, quality, value, price, etc. than B or 2) it is not worth doing B or it is not necessary to do B.

あの映画はとてもいいと聞いたので行ってみたが、みんなが<u>言うほどのことはなかった</u>。

Ano eiga wa totemo ii to kiita no de itte mita ga, minna ga iu hodo no koto wa nakatta.

Because I heard that the movie was very good, I went to see it, but it was not as good as they say.

落ち着きなさい。そんなに<u>大騒ぎするほどのことじゃない</u>でしょう。

Ochitsukinasai. Sonna ni ōsawagi suru hodo no koto ja nai deshō.

Calm down. It's not worth getting worked up about.

入院をしたと聞いたが、心配<u>するほどのことではなかった</u>。

Nyūin o shita to kiita ga, shinpai suru hodo no koto de wa nakatta.

I heard he was hospitalized, but it turned out to be nothing worth worrying about.

～かねる

～かねる is used in formal situations, and the speaker is indicating that what you have asked is difficult to do under the circumstances, even with the best will.

すみません。私ではちょっと分かり<u>かねます</u>ので、係の
者にお聞きください。

*Sumimasen. Watashi de wa chotto wakarikanemasu no
de, kakari no mono ni okiki kudasai.*

I am sorry, but I'm afraid I really don't know. Please ask
the clerk in charge.

とは～ないまでも

とは～ないまでも is often used with an expression like せ
めて (see also せめて) or ぐらい to show the speaker's minimal wish, desire, or request. The noun preceding this
phrase represents the speaker's maximum or even unreal-
istic desires etc.

世界旅行<u>とはいかないまでも</u>、せめて日本一周旅行ぐら
いはしたいものだ。

*Sekai-ryokō to wa ikanai made mo, semete Nihon isshū
ryokō gurai wa shitai mono da.*

Without even thinking of a world tour, I would at least
like to make a trip around Japan.

A<u>とはいかないまでも</u>、せめてBぐらいは取れるように
勉強しなさい。

*A to wa ikanai made mo, semete B gurai wa toreru yō ni
benkyō shinasai.*

Without even mentioning an A, at least study hard
enough to get a B.

いうまでもない

This phrase indicates that some action is to be taken for
granted and is often translated "it goes without saying" or
"needless to say." It is also used as an adverbial phrase: i.e.,
いうまでもなく.

これに消費税が加算されることは、<u>いうまでもないこと
です／いうまでもありません</u>。

Kore ni shōhi-zei ga kasan sareru koto wa, iu made mo nai koto desu/iu made mo arimasen.

It goes without saying that consumption tax will be added to this.

いうまでもなく、これには消費税が加算されます。

Iu made mo naku, kore ni wa shōhi-zei ga kasan saremasu.

Needless to say, consumption tax will be added to this.

Noun + たる

This phrase is usually used as part of a modifier of a following noun. It tends to be used in more elevated speech or writing.

悠々たる(としている)、アマゾン川の流れ

yūyū taru (to shite iru), Amazon-gawa no nagare

the vast and leisurely flowing Amazon River

親たる(である)者の責任が何か、彼には分かっていないようだ。

Oya taru (de aru) mono no sekinin ga nani ka, kare ni wa wakatte inai yō da.

It seems that he doesn't realize what a parent's responsibilities are.

Aにかけては

A にかけては is used to introduce the subject's special talent, notable characteristic, strong point, and so on. A is the topic in question.

記憶力の良さにかけては、彼は抜群だ。

Kioku-ryoku no yosa ni kakete wa, kare wa batsugun da.

When it comes to a good memory, he stands above the crowd.

がめついことにかけては、田中くんの右に出る者はいな
いよ。

*Gametsui koto ni kakete wa, Tanaka-kun no migi ni deru
mono wa inai yo.*

As for being greedy, Tanaka beats them all.

品質にかけては、このカメラが一番ですけど、こちらの
よりずっと高いんです。

*Hinshitsu ni kakete wa, kono kamera ga ichiban desu
kedo, kochira no yori zutto takai n' desu.*

As for quality, this camera is the best, but it is much
more expensive than this other one.

まして（や）／に（も）まして

まして (with や as optional) means "much more" in a positive sentence and "much less" in a negative one. It is a
conjunction and indicates that if A is so, then B, as a matter of course, must be more (or less) so.

まだ簡単な漢字も読めないんです。まして（や）新聞が読
めるわけがないでしょう。

*Mada kantan na kanji mo yomenai n' desu. Mashite (ya)
shinbun ga yomeru wake ga nai deshō.*

They can't even read simple kanji yet, so naturally they
can't read a newspaper.

動物の親でさえ、命をかけて子を守るという。まして人
間の親はそうあるべきだと思うのだけれど……。

*Dōbutsu no oya de sae, inochi o kakete ko o mamoru to
iu. Mashite ningen no oya wa sō aru beki da to omou
no da keredo …*

They say animals protect their young at the risk of their
lives. It goes without saying that human beings
should do the same, but …

に（も）まして is similar in meaning, but follows a noun and
means "even more than."

妹のジェニファは、姉の<u>アンナにもまして</u>美しい。

Imōto no Jenifa wa, ane no Anna ni mo mashite utsukushii.

The younger sister, Jennifer is even more beautiful than her older sister, Anna.

『<u>昨日にまして</u>、今日も（がんばろう）』というのが、あの人のモットーだそうだ。

"Kinō ni mashite, kyō mo (ganbarō)" to iu no ga, ano hito no mottō da sō da.

They say that his motto is "Even more than today, tomorrow, too (let's do our best)."

まして～をやである is a set phrase meaning "if that, then even more so this." It is often used in combination with さえ ("even").

彼は満足な仕事<u>さえ</u>与えられていない。<u>まして昇進をやである</u>。

Kare wa manzoku na shigoto sae ataerarete inai. Mashite shōshin o ya de aru.

He is not even assigned a decent job, so promotion is naturally out of question.

ことだ

ことだ is commonly used in conversation, to give advice or an order.

落第したくなかったら、もっと真剣に<u>勉強することだ</u>ね。

Rakudai shitaku nakattara, motto shinken ni benkyō suru koto da ne.

If you don't want to flunk the course, you should study harder (what you have to do is study more seriously).

旅行したければ、今から<u>貯金することです</u>。

Ryokō shitakereba, ima kara chokin suru koto desu.

If you want to travel, you should start saving now.

AにもBない

A is the volitional form of a verb (e.g., 行こう, 食べよう, or しよう) and B is a potential form of a verb (e.g., 行けない, 食べられない, or できない). The phrase indicates an impossible endeavor or desire that has been thwarted by circumstance.

こんな大降りじゃ、<u>出かけようにも出かけられない</u>わよ。

Konna ōburi ja, dekakeyō ni mo dakakerarenai wa yo.

With it raining this hard, there is no way we can go out.

ごめん。電話番号をどこかに置き忘れてしまったもんで<u>かけようにもかけられなかった</u>んだよ。

Gomen. Denwa-bangō o doko ka ni okiwasurete shimatta mon de kakeyō ni mo kakerarenakatta n' da yo.

Sorry. I left my address book somewhere, and so there was no way I could call you.

車が故障してしまって、迎えに<u>行こうにも行けなかった</u>んです。すみません。

Kuruma ga koshō shite shimatte, mukae ni ikō ni mo ikenakatta n' desu. Sumimasen.

Since my car broke down, it proved impossible to pick you up. I'm sorry.

〜たくても〜ない may replace this.

迎えに<u>行きたくても行けなかった</u>。

Mukae ni ikitakute mo ikenakatta.

I was unable to go to pick you up, even though I wanted to.

おいしそうだったから食べようと思ったんだけど、お腹が一杯で、<u>食べたくても食べられなかった</u>。

Oishisō datta kara tabeyō to omotta n' da kedo, onaka ga ippai de, tabetakute mo taberarenakatta.

It looked so delicious that I wanted to eat some, but I couldn't because I was full.

といったら

といったら is used to intensify the previous word, which is a nominalized form of an adjectival word with the さ ending.

> 山陰地方に行ってきたんだけどね、あの辺りのお魚のおいしさもさることながら、その<u>新鮮さと言ったら</u>。もう最高。
>
> *Sanin-chihō ni itte kita n' da kedo ne, ano atari no osakana no oishisa mo saru koto nagara, sono shinsensa to ittara. Mō saikō.*
>
> I went to the San'in region (along the Japan Sea coast), and the fish there—it goes without saying—are delicious, but, my, the freshness! It's out of this world.

In place of といったら, ったら may be used.

> 昨日親知らずを抜かれちゃったんだけど、<u>その痛さったら</u>、気が遠くなりそうだったわ。
>
> *Kinō oyashirazu o nukarechatta n' da kedo, sono itasa ttara, ki ga tōku narisō datta wa.*
>
> Yesterday I had a wisdom tooth pulled. My, did it hurt! I thought I was going to faint.

AもさることながらB

A もさることながら B is a set phrase meaning "A is true as expected, but B is also true." It is used to bring attention to the B statement, where the particle も is usually used.

> 彼は、<u>芸術的才能も</u>さることながら、学術的才能に<u>も</u>恵まれている。
>
> *Kare wa, gējutsu-teki sainō mo saru koto nagara, gakujutsu-teki sainō ni mo megumarete iru.*
>
> Not to mention his artistic talents, he is also blessed with scholastic ability.

> あのコンテスタントは、<u>美しさも</u>さることながら、学業の面で<u>も</u>、群を抜いていた。
>
> *Ano kontesutanto wa, utsukushisa mo saru koto nagara, gakugyō no men de mo, gun o nuite ita.*

The contestant was not only beautiful, but she was head and shoulders above the others in scholarly achievement.

挙げ句（に）／末（に）

末（すえ）（に）X and 挙げ句（あげく）（に）X focus on an outcome or result. In the case of 末（に）X, X is an outcome or the result of continuous trial, effort, lengthy waiting, or the like. It is often used with expressions such as つい に, やっぱり, and 何度（なんど）も. X, the outcome, may not be desirable or favorable. If it is not, then 挙げ句（に）X may replace it. In other words, 末（に）may indicate either desirable or undesirable results, but 挙げ句（に）always indicates a outcome or result that is negative or undesirable. An adverb such as さんざん is often used to reinforce this connotation. 挙げ句の果てにX is also used in the same situation for more emphasis.

考えに考えた末、やっぱり断ることにした。

Kangae ni kangaeta sue, yappari kotowaru koto ni shita.

Having thought it over and over, I decided to decline after all.

彼は、長年苦労した末に、ついに事業に成功した。

Kare wa, naganen kurō shita sue ni, tsui ni jigyō ni seikō shita.

After years of hardship, he finally achieved success in his business.

何度も失敗を繰り返しながら努力した末に、やっと一人 前の仕事ができるようになりました。

Nando mo shippai o kurikaeshinagara doryoku shita sue ni, yatto ichininmae no shigoto ga dekiru yō ni narimashita.

In the end, after sticking it out through repeated failure, I have finally reached the point where I can do a competent job.

さんざん<u>待たせた末に／挙げ句</u>、食事代まで人に払わせた。

Sanzan mataseta sue ni/ageku, shokuji-dai made hito ni harawaseta.

After keeping me waiting forever, he had me pay for the meal on top of it all.

彼女は、さんざん嫌味を<u>言った挙げ句</u>、出ていってしまった。

Kanojo wa, sanzan iyami o itta ageku, dete itte shimatta.

After making all kinds of sarcastic remarks, she just up and left.

彼は、事業に失敗し財産を<u>使い果たした挙げ句の果てに</u>、家族にも見捨てられてしまい、絶望的になっている。

Kare wa jigyō ni shippai shi, zaisan o tsukaihatashita ageku no hate ni, kazoku ni mo misuterarete shimai, zetsubō-teki ni natte iru.

He is in the depths of despair, due to the fact that after failing in business and exhausting his assets, even his family left him.

Index of Japanese Words and Phrases
(given in order of the hiragana syllabary)

よ

よっぽど, 102
よほど, 102

ら

らしい, 93

れ

例の, 15

わ

わざわざ, 101
煩わしい, 98

ん

んだ, 74
んだけど, 76
んです, 74
んですが, 76

（新装版）辞書では解らない慣用表現
Japanese Core Words and Phrases

2001 年 5 月　第 1 刷発行
2007 年 9 月　第 8 刷発行

著　者　　庄司香久子

発行者　　富田　充

発行所　　講談社インターナショナル株式会社
　　　　　〒112-8652　東京都文京区音羽 1-17-14
　　　　　電話　03-3944-6493（編集部）
　　　　　　　　03-3944-6492（マーケティング部・業務部）
　　　　　ホームページ　www.kodansha-intl.com

印刷・製本所　大日本印刷株式会社

JAPANESE LANGUAGE GUIDES

Easy-to-use guides to essential language skills

ALL ABOUT PARTICLES 新装版 助詞で変わるあなたの日本語 *Naoko Chino*

The most common and less common particles brought together and broken down into some 200 usages, with abundant sample sentences.

Paperback, 160 pages, ISBN 978-4-7700-2781-8

HOW TO TELL THE DIFFERENCE BETWEEN JAPANESE PARTICLES

Comparisons and Exercises 比べて分かる日本語の助詞 *Naoko Chino*

By grouping particles that are similar in function, this book helps students pin down differences in usage that would ordinarily take years to master. Definitions, sample sentences, usage notes, and quizzes enable students to move to a higher level of comprehension.

Paperback, 200 pages, ISBN 978-4-7700-2200-4

JAPANESE VERBS AT A GLANCE 新装版 日本語の動詞 *Naoko Chino*

Clear and straightforward explanations of Japanese verbs—their functions, forms, roles, and politeness levels.

Paperback, 180 pages, ISBN 978-4-7700-2765-8

BEYOND POLITE JAPANESE: A Dictionary of Japanese Slang and Colloquialisms

新装版 役に立つ話しことば辞典 *Akihiko Yonekawa*

Expressions that all Japanese, but few foreigners, know and use every day. Sample sentences for every entry.

Paperback, 176 pages, ISBN 978-4- 7700-2773-3

JAPANESE SENTENCE PATTERNS FOR EFFECTIVE COMMUNICATION

A Self-Study Course and Reference 日本語文型ハンドブック *Taeko Kamiya*

Presents 142 essential sentence patterns for daily conversation—all the ones an intermediate student should know, and all the ones a beginner should study to become minimally proficient in speaking. All in a handy, step-by-step format with pattern practice every few pages.

Paperback, 368 pages, ISBN 978-4-7700-2983-6

THE HANDBOOK OF JAPANESE VERBS 日本語動詞ハンドブック *Taeko Kamiya*

An indispensable reference and guide to Japanese verbs aimed at beginning and intermediate students. Precisely the book that verb-challenged students have been looking for.

• Verbs are grouped, conjugated, and combined with auxiliaries
• Different forms are used in sentences   • Each form is followed by reinforcing examples and exercises

Paperback, 256 pages, ISBN 978-4-7700-2683-5

THE HANDBOOK OF JAPANESE ADJECTIVES AND ADVERBS

日本語形容詞・副詞ハンドブック *Taeko Kamiya*

The ultimate reference manual for those seeking a deeper understanding of Japanese adjectives and adverbs and how they are used in sentences. Ideal, too, for those simply wishing to expand their vocabulary or speak livelier Japanese.

Paperback, 336 pages, ISBN 978-4-7700-2879-2

KODANSHA INTERNATIONAL DICTIONARIES

Easy-to-use dictionaries designed for learners of Japanese.

KODANSHA'S COMMUNICATIVE ENGLISH-JAPANESE DICTIONARY

日本語学習 英和辞典

A practical and comprehensive reference for learners at all levels.
• 22,000 entries and 19,000 example sentences and phrases
• Natural and accurate Japanese translations
• Japanese script throughout, with pronunciation of all kanji shown in hiragana or katakana
• Special columns on usage that teach you how to express yourself in Japanese
• Illustrations of objects, places, and people with parts labeled

Paperback, 1200 pages, ISBN 978-4-7700-1808-3

KODANSHA'S FURIGANA JAPANESE DICTIONARY

JAPANESE-ENGLISH / ENGLISH-JAPANESE ふりがな和英・英和辞典

Both of Kodansha's popular furigana dictionaries in one portable, affordable volume. A truly comprehensive and practical dictionary for English-speaking learners, and an invaluable guide to using the Japanese language.
• 30,000-word basic vocabulary   • Hundreds of special words, names, and phrases
• Clear explanations of semantic and usage differences   • Special information on grammar and usage

Hardcover, 1318 pages, ISBN 978-4-7700-2480-0

KODANSHA'S FURIGANA JAPANESE-ENGLISH DICTIONARY

新装版 ふりがな和英辞典

The essential dictionary for all students of Japanese.
• Furigana readings added to all *kanji*   • 16,000-word basic vocabulary

Paperback, 592 pages, ISBN 978-4-7700-2750-4

KODANSHA'S FURIGANA ENGLISH-JAPANESE DICTIONARY

新装版 ふりがな英和辞典

The companion to the essential dictionary for all students of Japanese.
• Furigana readings added to all *kanji*   • 14,000-word basic vocabulary

Paperback, 728 pages, ISBN 978-4-7700-2751-1

KODANSHA'S ROMANIZED JAPANESE-ENGLISH DICTIONARY

新装版 ローマ字和英辞典

A portable reference written for beginning and intermediate students.
• 16,000-word basic vocabulary   • No knowledge of *kanji* necessary

Paperback, 688 pages, ISBN 978-4-7700-2753-5

KODANSHA'S BASIC ENGLISH-JAPANESE DICTIONARY

日本語学習 基礎英日辞典

An annotated dictionary useful for both students and teachers.
• Over 4,500 headwords and 18,000 vocabulary items
• Examples and information on stylistic differences
• Appendices for technical terms, syntax and grammar

Paperback, 1520 pages, ISBN 978-4-7700-2895-2

KODANSHA INTERNATIONAL DICTIONARIES
Easy-to-use dictionaries designed for learners of Japanese.

THE KODANSHA KANJI LEARNER'S DICTIONARY
新装版 漢英学習字典
The perfect kanji tool for beginners to advanced learners.
• Revolutionary SKIP lookup method • Five lookup methods and three indices
• 2,230 entries and 41,000 meanings for 31,000 words
Paperback, 1060 pages (2-color), ISBN 978-4-7700-2855-6

KODANSHA'S ESSENTIAL KANJI DICTIONARY
新装版 常用漢英熟語辞典
A functional character dictionary that is both compact and comprehensive.
• Complete guide to the 1,945 essential *jōyō kanji* • 20,000 common compounds
• Three indices for finding *kanji*
Paperback, 928 pages, ISBN 978-4-7700-2891-4

KODANSHA'S EFFECTIVE JAPANESE USAGE DICTIONARY
新装版 日本語使い分け辞典
A concise, bilingual dictionary which clarifies the usage of frequently confused words and phrases.
• Explanations of 708 synonymous terms • Numerous example sentences
Paperback, 768 pages, ISBN 978-4-7700-2850-1

KODANSHA'S DICTIONARY OF BASIC JAPANESE IDIOMS
日本語イディオム辞典
All idioms are given in Japanese script and romanized text with English translations. There are
approximately 880 entries, many of which have several senses.
Paperback, 672 pages, ISBN 978-4-7700-2797-9

A DICTIONARY OF BASIC JAPANESE SENTENCE PATTERNS
日本語基本文型辞典
Author of the best-selling All About Particles explains fifty of the most common, basic patterns
and their variations, along with numerous contextual examples. Both a reference and a textbook
for students at all levels.
• Formulas delineating basic pattern structure • Commentary on individual usages
Paperback, 320 pages, ISBN 978-4-7700-2608-8

A DICTIONARY OF JAPANESE PARTICLES
てにをは辞典
Treats over 100 particles in alphabetical order, providing sample sentences for each meaning.
• Meets students' needs from beginning to advanced levels
• Treats principal particle meanings as well as variants
Paperback, 368 pages, ISBN 978-4-7700-2352-0

JAPANESE LANGUAGE GUIDES
Easy-to-use guides to essential language skills

13 SECRETS FOR SPEAKING FLUENT JAPANESE
日本語をペラペラ話すための13の秘訣　*Giles Murray*

The most fun, rewarding, and universal techniques of successful learners of Japanese that anyone can put immediately to use. A unique and exciting alternative, full of lively commentaries, comical illustrations, and brain-teasing puzzles.
Paperback, 184 pages, ISBN 978-4-7700-2302-5

BREAKING INTO JAPANESE LITERATURE: Seven Modern Classics in Parallel Text
日本語を読むための七つの物語　*Giles Murray*

Read classics of modern Japanese fiction in the original with the aid of a built-in, customized dictionary, free MP3 sound files of professional Japanese narrators reading the stories, and literal English translations. Features Ryunosuke Akutagawa's "Rashomon" and other stories.
Paperback, 240 pages, ISBN 978-4-7700-2899-0

EXPLORING JAPANESE LITERATURE:
Read Mishima, Tanizaki and Kawabata in the Original
日本語を読むための三つの物語　三島・谷崎・川端　*Giles Murray*

Provides all the backup you need to enjoy three works of modern Japanese fiction in the original language: Yukio Mishima's "Patriotism," Jun'ichiro Tanizaki's "The Secret," and Yasunari Kawabata's "Snow Country Miniature."
Paperback, 352 pages; ISBN 978-4-7700-3041-2

BREAKTHROUGH JAPANESE: 20 Mini Lessons for Better Conversation
日本語をネイティブのように話す秘訣　*Hitomi Hirayama*

A lively book that amplifies and reinforces the skills gained from more conventional textbooks. Designed to stimulate or rekindle a learner's curiosity, it is packed with activities that make language speaking fun. For all levels.
Paperback, 176 pages, ISBN 978-4-7700-2873-0

MAKING SENSE OF JAPANESE: What the Textbooks Don't Tell You
新装版 日本語の秘訣　*Jay Rubin*

"Brief, wittily written essays that gamely attempt to explain some of the more frustrating hurdles [of Japanese].… They can be read and enjoyed by students at any level." —*Asahi Evening News*
Paperback, 144 pages, ISBN 978-4-7700-2802-4

BASIC CONNECTIONS: Making Your Japanese Flow
新装版 日本語の基礎ルール　*Kakuko Shoji*

Explains how words and phrases dovetail, how clauses pair up with other clauses, how sentences come together to create harmonious paragraphs. The goal is to enable the student to speak both coherently and smoothly.
Paperback, 160 pages, ISBN 978-4-7700-2860-0

JAPANESE CORE WORDS AND PHRASES: Things You Can't Find in a Dictionary
新装版 辞書では解らない慣用表現　*Kakuko Shoji*

Some Japanese words and phrases, even though they lie at the core of the language, forever elude the student's grasp. This book brings these recalcitrants to bay.
Paperback, 144 pages, ISBN 978-4-7700-2774-0